Miranda Hall

# Packed Lunches
## and Picnics

*Other Books by Miranda Hall*
FEEDING YOUR CHILDREN

Miranda Hall

# Packed Lunches
## and Picnics

PIATKUS

© 1985 Miranda Hall
First published in 1985 by
Judy Piatkus (Publishers) Ltd, London

British Library Cataloguing in Publication Data

Hall, Miranda
  Packed lunches.
  1. Lunchbox cookery
  I. Title
  641.5'3      TX735

  ISBN 0-86188-332-2
  ISBN 0-86188-338-1 Pbk

Edited by Susan Fleming
Designed by Paul Saunders

Typeset by Phoenix Photosetting, Chatham
Printed and bound by Mackays of Chatham Ltd

# Contents

**Introduction**   6

**Packed Lunches**   14

For Small Children   17

For Older Children and Students   32

Desk-Top Dining   52

**Picnics**   70

Family Picnics   72

Children's Picnic Parties   80

Moveable Feasts   87

Index   95

# Introduction

Packed lunches and picnics are both meals to be eaten away from home, and they must therefore consist of foods which are portable. To many busy mums, this means sandwiches, packets of crisps or wrapped biscuits, but today, with the advent of more sophisticated methods of packaging, shortcuts like these are entirely unnecessary. If you want to have hot soups, jacket potatoes or casseroles, prawns in aspic, warm flans, crisp chilled salad or ice cream, you can now confidently plan to have all these in your lunch box or food flask – and throughout this book you'll get many ideas and tips for nutritious and tasty foods to suit all age groups.

Packed lunches are usually for one person only, and it must always be remembered that this meal should provide one-third of the child or adult's daily requirements of nutrients – protein, vitamins, fibre, etc. A picnic, on the other hand, is a treat, a special occasion, a party, a moveable feast, when you can let caution blow to the winds and indulge yourself, your friends and your family.

The following notes on packaging, and all the recipe ideas will, I hope, inspire you to create many delicious packed lunches and picnics. Do not forget, though – the most important aspect of portable meals – that they should look really tempting: the food should look as good when finally eaten as it did when it left the kitchen.

## Packaging Equipment

The most basic of requirements are aluminium foil, clingfilm and plastic food bags.

They are inexpensive, hygienic, and a boon for the packed luncher and picnicker – and the packer! Other equipment is vital too, and the following list should be useful.

**Vacuum Flasks** These are designed to keep drinks and soup hot or chilled, and are invaluable for portable meals. There are basically three types. The all-plastic unbreakable Thermos (with foam insulation) is designed with children in mind, many to fit a child's lunch box. Some may come with a screw top incorporating a flip-up spout for easy drinking, and with a warning not to use for drinks that are too hot which might burn if gulped down. In fact, drinks in this type of flask cool comparatively quickly. A boiling liquid poured in at breakfast time will be barely hot (around 100°F/37°C) 4 hours later at lunch time – an acceptable temperature for a child's drink or soup, but not for most adults who like a really hot cup of coffee. These Thermoses usually hold ½ pint (300 ml), but may come with a very small cup, so make sure that five to six year olds practise pouring out at home first so that they learn how to pour without over-filling.

The traditional vacuum flask has a breakable but replaceable silvered lining. They are still the most efficient at conserving heat, keeping drinks piping hot (about 150°F/65°C) well past the 4–5 hours normally required. This would be too hot for safety for small children, and also too delicate for use in packed school lunches. The smallest size holds about 8 fl. oz (225 ml) – a cupful. Some might find this insufficient and prefer a 12 fl. oz (350 ml) size.

The wide-necked plastic-lined flask is the

7

most versatile of all, and is often called a food flask. It is not quite so efficient at retaining hot (about 130°F/54°C after 4 hours) and cold temperatures as the traditional flask – where food is in direct contact with the vacuum lining – but it is more than adequate for a 4–5 hour period. It is good for a wide range of hot and cold foods and drinks – also excellent for making yogurt or storing ice cubes for drinks parties at home. If a food flask breaks the food remains free of glass, but the flasks may be too chunky to fit neatly into a briefcase for those who wish to take their lunch discreetly to the office.

**Lunch Boxes** These are well designed, easy to carry and practical for a child's school lunch. Most are large enough to pack in quite a substantial meal. Pick a design on the outside that will still be acceptable as the child grows older. A lunch box which has its own Thermos will give you the best use of available space.

**Insulated or Chill Boxes and Bags** These are good for picnics (and useful when defrosting the freezer). The bags are the most versatile, doubling as insulated containers when shopping for frozen foods. Light and easy to carry, they are ideal if you shop in your lunch break or have a long journey home. Choose bags that have thick, well insulated walls, good handles that will not break when the bag is full, and with a large zip opening so that larger items can be put in with ease.

Insulated boxes provide greater protection when packing crushable items, and some are now designed to carry bottles upright, a useful feature if you are regularly taking several wine bottles to a picnic.

Although normally only used to keep food chilled, both boxes and bags can be used to keep food frozen for 3–4 hours, especially if frozen ice packs are used. The bags and boxes may also be used to keep food hot – first wrap food in foil then in towels or newspapers. Obviously only fill bag or box with hot *or* cold items!

**Picnic Hampers** These are lovely to own if you want to have a stylish picnic, but you may find the hamper restricts your choice of food if you try to pack everything inside. It's certainly very cumbersome to store. Give priority space to the safe packing of wine glasses for a special occasion. Food can always go in other containers.

**Picnic Paper and Plastic Ware** There is an excellent range of paper ware – matching napkins, tablecloths, paper plates, bowls and cups. Nevertheless, most people find the paper cups only suitable for children: they are not ideal for hot coffee or soup, a plastic cup with handle is more comfortable; neither are they acceptable for wine. If real glasses are not practical, perspex or clear plastic beakers are a good substitute. For regular picnickers or packed lunchers, good quality plastic ware – plates, bowls and mugs – will be a good investment. These can match napkins, cloths, etc, for a well coordinated look. (Avoid blue items, though, which are unflattering for food.)

For packed lunches and informal picnics it it often easier to eat straight out of plastic bowls and boxes with snap-on lids. Buy good quality plastics in the more expensive ranges, Tupperware, for instance, which will be air/watertight. For packed lunches it may be wiser to buy a variety of colours so that the family's lunches can be colour coded to avoid unwelcome surprises on the desk top if the wrong box is picked up!

**Cutlery** Most packed lunch and picnic eaters seem to prefer to use their fingers as much as possible – especially younger children – but spoons, forks and knives do widen the range of food you can serve. You have the choice of cheap disposable plastic ware, strong plastic cutlery, or household cutlery. The disposable plastic ware is very flimsy – the knife and fork suitable for salad but hopeless for firmer meats. The strong plastic cutlery is certainly much easier and more comfortable to use, and will last quite a long time, but the knives of most are only moderately good at cutting meat.

When it comes to serving pâtés, flans, cakes, bread, fruit, etc, a really good kitchen or serrated knife is essential at a picnic (push a cork on the tip if pointed for safety in transportation). At formal picnics, especially where everyone is seated at a table, it is much pleasanter to use real cutlery.

## Packing Food for Transport

**Soups and Drinks** Hot drinks and soups should be heated only 4–5 hours before required if they are to be enjoyed hot. To improve heat retention, rinse vacuum flask with boiling water first. Tea should have cold milk transported in a separate small screw-top bottle, or the flavour will spoil. For soups, prepare well in advance: if wished, freeze in one-portion quantities – 5–7 fl. oz (150–200 ml) for a small child, 10–15 oz (300–425 ml) for larger appetites. Thaw soup overnight in fridge for one portion quantities, longer for larger quantities, then bring to boil at breakfast for packed lunch. Avoid soups with high milk content which are less stable to freeze and may curdle slightly with acid vegetables (onion or watercress, for instance) if kept hot for long periods.

For cold drinks, pack scissors to open large 1¾ pint (1 litre) cartons of fruit juice. The small ones (sizes vary) come with a straw and an easy-to-pierce hole, which are practical but less economical to use. Flavoured milks and milk shakes are best served chilled so place in fridge then transport in Thermos flasks, screw-top bottles or a watertight covered mug, in an insulated box or bag. For those wishing to recycle packaging, the plastic screw-top pop and squash bottles are useful for refilling for picnics. Glass bottles are not suitable for children unless under careful adult supervision.

Wine cartons are easier if less aesthetic than bottles to transport for picnics. The small wine cartons are ideal for the indulgent desk-top diner or cautious drivers who are picnicking. They save the trouble of packing a corkscrew and are lighter and safer for hikers and bikers. For large picnic parties wine boxes are very handy if there is a car tail-gate, hamper, chill box, table or handy wall to rest them on while dispensing. One 1¾ pint (1 litre) carton serves 8 glasses.

**Sandwiches** Sandwiches containing salad items are best made on the day they will be eaten. Most others can be prepared either the night before and stored overnight in the

fridge or, if preferred, can be frozen. When freezing sandwiches, wrap singly in freezer clingfilm so that the desired quantity can be taken out to thaw evenly overnight in the fridge. Batches of frozen wrapped sandwiches should be placed in labelled polythene bags or boxes for extra protection and easy identification. A large loaf will make over one dozen rounds, a small loaf about seven. Sandwiches prepared to store overnight or for immediate transportation can be foil wrapped or placed in small polythene bags, although clingfilm is cheaper to use and makes food look more tempting. Where sandwiches have soft fillings – well filled with salad, for instance – it can be useful to pack them on small polystyrene trays (re-cycled from supermarket packaging) before wrapping securely in clingfilm to ensure that they still look tidy when eaten. Rolled sandwiches can be packed on trays, or individually wrapped in clingfilm as you roll them up, then should be packed in small plastic boxes for transportation.

To ensure sandwiches always arrive in good condition pack in plastic boxes. For packed lunches, small boxes of about 5½ × 4½ inches (14 × 11 cm) are the perfect size for large slices of bread made into sandwiches or halved pitta breads. Smaller boxes of 4 inches (10 cm) square are ideal for small sandwiches made from small loaves. Oblong margarine cartons can be used if sandwiches are halved and stacked on top of each other. For children, even if sandwiches are to be placed in a lunch box, it is often wise to give them the protection of a plastic box, as they can get very shaken up with other contents. Bread rolls are usually firmer to pack so wrap

well in clingfilm or foil, or slip in a small polythene bag.

**Spreads and Dips**  Both sweet and savoury may be made in advance. Firm meat spreads and fish spreads made from tinned or smoked fish can be made in advance and frozen. Cheese, lentil and nut spreads and dips will store in the fridge for 2–3 days, but nut butters can be stored for a month at least if nuts, oil, sugar and honey are their only contents. Most fruit and vegetable spreads and dips are best used within 24 hours.

Spreads are likely to be used as sandwich fillings but where these are soft enough they are particularly popular with children and the weight-conscious to use as dips. Turn into plastic cartons – 4–5 oz (115–150 g) cottage cheese or cream cartons are a good size – or, for adults, small honey or dumpy tomato purée jars. Pack with a small bag or clingfilm-wrapped bundle of vegetables or fruits to dunk in mixture. Soft dips are best not frozen as the fat and water content tend to separate and the pleasant creamy texture is lost.

**Salad and Vegetables**  For all packed lunches, salad items are best transported in a polythene box for protection unless very firm. All leafy green salads should be packed without a dressing so that they do not go mushy. You can use any plastic or re-cycled margarine cartons – the shallow firm 8.8 oz (250 g) sunflower margarine cartons being a particularly good shape to eat from – and they pack in a briefcase or satchel. Potato, rice and pasta salads, coleslaw, tomato and other mixed salads containing cooked and raw ingredients are likely to be tossed in a dressing before packing so need to be in watertight plastic containers to prevent seepage. For a picnic you may be able to guarantee these will not be tipped in transport, in which case any lidded carton would be adequate.

At informal picnics you may like to pack salad items in bags – washed lettuce in one, tomatoes, cucumber in others and place all in an insulated box or bag to divide out later, but it will usually be quicker and simpler to have individual cartons of salad for each picnicker.

Dressings for green salads need packing separately for packed-lunch eaters and picnickers alike – in small plastic pots or glass mustard jars. The lids need to be both watertight and made of plastic or plastic-lined metal (for metal rusts in contact with vinegar). Pickles, chutneys, mayonnaise and mustard are all most welcome at picnics: tubes of mustard are particularly easy to pack, other items can be packed as for dressings.

Limp lettuce is never very exciting. If you cannot keep this item cool in an insulated bag or box it is better to avoid it in favour of crisper salad ingredients – cabbage, Chinese leaves, Webb and iceberg lettuces.

Avocados are delicious for a picnic. Halve at your destination, so pack a knife as well as spoons for eating them. For a packed lunch, the discoloration of a cut avocado is easy to solve. Cut avocado at breakfast, lift out stone, set on dishcloth to steady and split in half with heavy knife tapped with a hammer or rolling pin. Return split stone to avocado and wrap tightly with clingfilm. The stone will discolour (discard at lunch), but the flesh will not.

A good range of cooked vegetables can be used for picnics. Some – such as carrots, peas, sweetcorn, peppers, parsnip, beetroot, the entire bean family (both fresh and dried), continental lentils plus also rice and pasta, but not potatoes – can be frozen ready to bring out, thaw overnight and toss with a variety of dressings, herbs, pickles and relishes to make quick and interesting salads. Plainly boiled pasta left from a meal should be lightly tossed in oil to prevent sticking, then used the next day as the basis of a salad. All these are especially useful for interesting packed lunches in winter months when many traditional salad items are expensive or tasteless.

**Made-Up Dishes** Pâtés and savoury or meat loaves are excellent for packed lunches. Double the recipe to make surplus from a family meal or prepare just for picnics or packed lunches. Wrap slices in clingfilm, place in named and dated bag, then freeze for later use (within approximately 1 month). For picnics, transport pâtés and meat loaves in their baking trays or dishes if possible. If you don't have the flat pack (collapsible) loaf tins, turn your pâtés and loaves out at home, wash tin or dish, line with foil or clingfilm, and return food to it. The food will then be easy to lift out later.

With the use of a wide-necked Thermos, casseroles and the thick soups and chowders are most welcome for packed lunches and shooting or other winter picnics. Prepare in advance and freeze if wished, in handy-sized portions, if for packed lunches. Thaw over-

night and bring to the boil before turning into wide-necked Thermos. Omit such ingredients as fish, shellfish, green leafy vegetable (e.g. sprouts and cabbage), also white rice and pasta – which go mushy or spoil if kept hot. Combinations of all root and pulse vegetables (beans and lentils), white and red cabbage, are very good and tasty, with or without meats.

**Pies and Flans** All pastries are at their crispest and best if freshly cooked – within 24 hours – so, for packed lunches especially, do consider whether pies and flans can be baked while you are cooking an evening meal to cool overnight for a packed lunch next day. Pies, quiches and other flans can be made in individual large 4 inch (10 cm) tart-let tins, or Yorkshire pudding tins for packed lunch portions. But they can also be frozen raw in their tins, then knocked out and stored again, well wrapped, in the freezer. Place in the same tins to cook from frozen. Pack in their tins wrapped in clingfilm for safe transport. Large flans and pies cooked in round, square or oblong tins can be cut in portions, wrapped when cold, then frozen for later packed meals or picnics. Savoury pies and flans are best only frozen for 1 month, fruit pies can be frozen for up to 3 months.

For big picnic parties large tarts and flans are best transported in tins. Use a loose-bottomed flan ring if you have one for easy serving. Savoury quiches are delicious warm so put one freshly baked in an insulated bag (cool for 15 minutes first). Keeping warm is not recommended for prawn and other shell-fish quiches.

**Cakes and Loaves** Cakes, buns and a wide variety of fruit, malt and nut loaves, freeze beautifully. For packed lunches make cakes in 7–8 inch (17.5–20 cm) tins then cut in wedges to fit in sandwich boxes, or bake in roasting tins or similar for slabs to cut into squares or fingers. Loaves are particularly easy to slice, wrap and pack in small boxes. Cakes, loaves and buns which will not be eaten within 2–4 days are best bagged and frozen as soon as they are cool. Cakes and loaves should be sliced, individually wrapped, then frozen and put in bags or boxes in the freezer. For buns, open-freeze on trays then store in bags. Bring out and thaw in the quantities required.

For picnics, cakes can be taken freshly baked either in the tin in which they were baked – spring-clip cake tins are best for easy turning out – or the cake can be turned out, decorated or filled, frozen if more convenient, then thawed and transported in air-tight cake box or tin. Only parkin and gingerbreads benefit from storing for 5–7 days before freezing.

**Fruit** Wash all fruit well for packed lunch and picnics, even if they are to be peeled, so that chemical sprays which may have been used do not get on the hands. Apples are easy, but most other fruits are best protected by a plastic box. Most cut fruit needs wrapping in clingfilm before placing in a box with a teaspoon. Soft fruit can go straight in a small box. Most lunch boxes provide enough protection for bananas, pears, peaches and citrus fruits. For picnics all fruits benefit by being transported chilled in an insulated box – especially melons.

**Puds** For packed lunches a good variety of desserts in the freezer are most useful. Fruit crumbles can be made in large dishes then spooned into individual small lidded cartons. Freeze any spare portions for future use. Mousses, cheesecakes, trifle and jellies all freeze well. Make them in small plastic-lidded containers. Banana should be avoided in fruit jellies as they discolour and go mushy. Stewed fruits, purées and fruit salads are all good for packed lunches and picnics. All need to go into watertight containers for safety. Fresh fruit salads are best not frozen, but those made from diced, tinned and cooked fruits plus plain stewed fruits and purées, all freeze well and are useful to have in plastic-lidded cartons. Do not over-fill cartons as they will expand during freezing.

---

### Freezing note

*Not suitable*
Whole or diced hard-boiled egg
Whole or diced potato
Raw salad items
Banana

*Freeze 1 month*
Savoury spreads
Pâtés, cold meats, smoked fish
Pastries, flans, quiche
Sandwiches
Bread
Casseroles

*Freeze 3 months*
Fruit drinks, fruit purées
Ice creams
Fruit pies, jellies, crumbles
Cooked beans and lentils
Cooked root vegetables other than potatoes
Cooked peppers and sweetcorn
Cooked rice
Cakes, buns, fruit loaves
Soups

---

# Packed Lunches

Packed lunches – whether for small or older schoolchildren, students or working adults – are one of the three main daily meals, and as such should aim to provide at least one-third of the daily nutritional needs of protein, vitamins, minerals, fibre and energy, etc. They will play a vital part in short- and long-term good health. Look at the chart on page 16, which is designed to help children and adults choose a nutritional and well balanced packed meal.

Packed meals can easily tend to be high in fat, sugar, salt and chemical additives, but low in food value unless food is chosen with care. The ubiquitous sandwich, although it can provide a nutritionally balanced packed meal, frequently provides too much fat because it is spread lavishly and often unnecessarily with butter and fatty fillings, and contains too little fibre. To solve this problem, select high-fibre breads (high-fibre white bread, with added bean fibre, may be more acceptable than wholemeal), and low-fat spreads like sunflower (low-cholesterol) margarine, or omit altogether. Choose the new low-fat hard and soft cheeses, lean meats and lots of salad and vegetable ingredients, and be generous with these fillings.

Do not necessarily think of bread as fattening: it is a good source of protein, fibre, vitamins and minerals, and not just calories. Look at the following sections and you will find many ideas for interesting sandwiches. When you are feeding teenagers or the ever-hungry who have high calorie needs, bread is in fact the healthiest source of calories. It's also one of the cheapest, so give plenty and choose a good variety: don't always serve convenient sliced breads, but a range of baps and rolls, French bread and pitta breads.

Try to avoid the easy options for packed lunches – all the junk foods like crisps, biscuits, sweets, pop, etc – which if eaten regularly or in quantity will damage the health. Children, teenagers and many adults so easily get into the habit – in fact, become quite addicted to eating them – and are unwittingly influenced by the advertising of these products. Just think, when did you last see an advert for apples? Vegetables and fruit are vital requirements for all, providing what we need daily for good health, and with today's packaging there is no reason why raw or cooked vegetables, salads and soups cannot be part of a packed meal. A good variety of healthy hot or cold drinks can also be useful.

Keep sweetened foods to a minimum. We are recommended for good health to keep sugar intake in all our food below 2 oz (60 g) per day, less for small children – about 4 level tablespoons. Much is disguised in what we eat and drink: there is 1 tablespoon per 5 oz (150 g) carton of yogurt, a lot in breakfast cereals, tinned soups, baked beans and other processed foods.

The recipes in the following packed lunch sections are chosen with the family's good health in mind especially, but many in the picnic sections will also be useful, and give you many different and exciting ideas. As a packed lunch is generally for one, if it is to be truly appreciated, the individual's tastes and preferences have to be taken into consideration: the contents need to be chosen with the individual diner in mind and they should be packed with the maximum eye appeal and variety of tastes and textures.

# Chart of Choices

If your family are faddy or fussy let them choose their own packed lunches using the following lists as a guide. Ensure a well balanced meal by choosing, for example, one item from each column at first then extra according to appetite. Vegetables for packed lunches can be given raw in pieces to eat in the fingers or cooked and combined in salads or in soups. Fruits, raw, cooked in mousses and jellies, or as dried fruits, are the perfect finish to any well-balanced meal. Yogurt can be a good addition to packed meals – one 5 oz (150 g) carton contains about 1 tablespoon of sugar and only about the same of fruit, but the low-fat milk content is useful.

| Protein food | Cereal | Vegetables | Fruit |
|---|---|---|---|
| Bacon | Bread rolls | Artichokes | Apple |
| Beef | Brown bread | Aubergines | Apricots |
| Cheese (hard) | Brown rice | Avocado | Bananas |
| Cheese (soft) | Biscuit (plain | Beansprouts | Blackcurrants |
| Chicken | wholemeal) | Beans | Cherries |
| Corned beef | French bread | Beetroot | Clementines |
| Egg | Fruit cake (plain) | Broccoli | Dates |
| Fish pâté | Fruit loaf | Brussels sprouts | Gooseberries |
| Ham | Granary bread | Cabbage | Grapes |
| Kidney | Malt loaf | Carrot | Grapefruit |
| Lamb | Muesli biscuit | Cauliflower | Kiwi fruit |
| Lentil pâté | Pasta | Celery | Melon |
| Liver pâté | Pastry | Chinese leaves | Nectarine |
| Nuts | Pitta bread | Courgettes | Oranges |
| Peanut butter | Pizza | Cucumber | Peach |
| Pork | Rye crisp breads | Fennel | Pears |
| Sardines | Scones | Lettuce | Pineapple |
| Sausage | Tea cakes | Mushrooms | Plums |
| Smoked mackerel | White bread | Parsnips | Raisins |
| Soya bean curd | Wholemeal crackers | Peas | Raspberries |
| Tuna | Wholemeal bread | Peppers | Rhubarb |
| | Wholemeal pastry | Potatoes | Satsumas |
| | | Onions | Sharon fruit |
| | | Radish | Strawberries |
| | | Sprouted seeds | Sultanas |
| | | Swede | Tangerines |
| | | Sweetcorn | Tomatoes |
| | | Watercress | |

# For Small Children

Lunch for small children is a most important meal if they are to have the stamina to cope with a busy day. For many parents, today's school dinners seem an unacceptable choice: poor value for money with poor quality of foods. This often leaves a packed lunch as the only practical – and healthy – alternative.

There are two important considerations regarding packed lunches for the younger child: they need to be nutritious and they need to be *eaten*! If a conservative fussy youngster wants only an egg sandwich and an apple daily, it may seem boringly repetitive to you, but at least it will supply many of the child's nutritional needs, and you can be confident it will be eaten. Unfortunately many young children – partly as a result of skilled advertising, and partly because manufacturers know how to take advantage of our children's weaknesses – clamour for a Coke, crisp and Kit-Kat type lunch endlessly. This will supply calories and chemicals only and few of the growing child's real needs.

Parents are faced with a dilemma. If you take an *eat-that-because-it's-good-for-you* approach you are unlikely to gain your child's unfailing cooperation. So to help both parent and child arrive at a practical and acceptable solution, with some variety, if possible, the chart on page 16 should prove particularly useful, listing ideas to achieve a balanced diet. These will supply a protein food, a carbohydrate food, a vegetable and fruit. The combination of these four will provide a really good range of vitamins, minerals and other essentials for good health plus energy. It will ensure the packed lunch is not too high in unhealthy fats, sugars and chemicals. Since children do not have an understanding of nutrition at this age it is unwise to allow them the responsibility of freely choosing just what they *want*. Guidance is important since the food intake, the *needs* and thus health of a growing child, are too important to be left to the child's own whim.

Many mothers find that if they allow their children any junk food – crisps, biscuits, cakes, sweets, pop, even if packed alongside more suitable foods – they can be confident of one thing only: the junk foods will be consumed first, and in the rush to get out to play you will never be sure whether the rest is eaten, given away or dumped in the bin. You need therefore to find tempting, but not time-consuming or costly, alternatives that will contribute more to your child's long-term good health. Nevertheless, rest assured that junior-school children are not prone to anorexia – they won't allow themselves to starve – so don't be afraid to only pack sensible foods that they *do* like. You can be sure they will eat something from pure natural hunger. Many will badger their parents for junk food saying 'But everyone takes crisps', claiming that no-one else eats raw carrots for lunch, but I can confidently deny this. An ever-increasing number of mothers have turned to *real food* recently, and are determined their children will not be junk-food addicts.

# Savoury Sandwiches

While some children like the same sort of lunch week in, week out, many need variety to stimulate their interest and appetite. The following combinations include many popular ingredients and will help you find imaginative ideas for the family.

**Lamb and pea** Spread bread with low-fat curd cheese mashed with cooked peas and mint. Fill with thinly sliced cold lamb.

**Russian beef pitta** Half a pitta bread filled with sliced corned beef and Russian salad (cooked, diced potato, carrot and beetroot in mayonnaise).

**Mortadella scone** Large cheese scone spread with ketchup, filled with sliced tomato (preferably the firm beefsteak variety) and Mortadella sausage.

**Bacon and bean bap** Chopped cooked broad or green bean mixed with cottage cheese in bap with grilled bacon.

**Cheese and cucumber roll** Low-fat Cheddar cheese in bread roll with chutney or pickle, plus sliced dill pickle or fresh cucumber.

**Cold pork and coleslaw** Wholemeal sandwich filled with cold pork, apple sauce and layer of coleslaw.

**Sardine and tomato sandwich** Mash a tin of sardines in tomato sauce to a smooth paste with grated lemon rind. Fill sandwich, adding sliced tomato.

**Crunchy bean, nut and curd** Spread sandwich with low-fat curd cheese, sprinkle with salted peanuts, and top with layer of bean-sprouts.

# Sweet Success Sandwiches

Many young children are reluctant to eat savoury sandwiches of meats and salads. They clamour for jam sandwiches leaving parents rightly concerned that they are not eating a well-balanced meal. The following ideas will help you solve this problem with confidence.

**Strawberry and quark** Wholemeal bread spread with strawberry jam, generously filled with plain Quark cheese.

**American favourite** White or brown bread spread thickly with peanut butter and sandwiched with raspberry jam.

**Lemon and walnut** Lemon curd, preferably home-made, spread on wholemeal bread and sprinkled with chopped walnuts.

**Sultana and apricot curd** Spread wholemeal scones amply with low-fat curd cheese, and sandwich with apricot jam and sultanas.

**Lime and Caerphilly** Spread high-fibre white bread with lime marmalade and sandwich with slice of Caerphilly cheese (or other firm mild cheese).

**Tongue and jelly** Spread tea cake with butter or margarine then redcurrant jelly. Fill with sliced tongue.

**Pickle and sausage** Spread high-fibre white bread with sweet pickle then roll up round a cooked cold sausage.

**Crunchy chocolate and banana** Spread bread with hazelnut and chocolate spread, sprinkle with chopped hazelnuts, and roll round small banana.

# Leek and Potato Soup

A delicious soup – a culinary classic too, as Vichysoisse – and very popular with small children. (But do call it potato soup if leeks are not a favourite vegetable!) Add extra dried milk to make it creamier and more nutritious for those with small appetites. Freeze if you wish in convenient portions. Thaw overnight and reheat at breakfast time, not quite to boiling. Send to school in an unbreakable vacuum flask with a mug or wide straw.

SERVES 8

**1 lb (450 g) leeks**
**8 oz (225 g) potatoes**
**2 oz (60 g) sunflower margarine**
**1¾ pints (1 litre) milk**
**Generous ½ pint (300 ml) chicken stock**
**4 tablespoons dried milk powder**
**1 teaspoon salt**

**1.** Split and wash the leeks well, then slice. Scrub the potatoes well rather than peeling them (most of the vitamin C lies just under the skin), then slice. Cook leeks and potatoes together slowly in melted margarine in a covered pan for 10 minutes, without browning.
**2.** Stir in milk, stock, milk powder and salt. Simmer for 15 minutes or until potatoes and leeks are soft. Purée very finely until really smooth and velvety.

# Chicken Liver Spread

Pâté may be used as a dip for salad items, or as a sandwich filling. If you wish to freeze it after cooking, drop in large spoonfuls (or pipe it) on a baking tray and open-freeze before storing in a polythene bag. These blobs make for handy portions, and thaw quickly.

For serving as a dip, pack in a small carton and accompany it with sticks of raw carrot and cucumber, florets of raw cauliflower, small savoury biscuits or fingers of wholemeal bread baked until crisp.

MAKES ABOUT 12 oz (350 g)

**8 oz (225 g) frozen chicken livers**
**4 rashers streaky bacon**
**3 oz (90 g) sunflower margarine**
**2 tablespoons tomato purée**
**Salt and pepper**

**1.** Thaw chicken livers and cut out any greenish parts – these may be bitter. Use scissors to cut rind off the bacon, then cut rashers into small pieces. Fry liver and bacon in margarine until golden and the liver is just firm.
**2.** Purée all finely together in a food processor or electric blender, adding tomato purée, then season to taste and turn into one or more containers. Cover tightly with clingfilm or, if you wish to store it in the fridge for a few days, cover with a little melted butter or margarine.

# Home-Made Peanut Butter

Many children do not like the tacky, roof-of-the-mouth-clinging texture of commercial peanut butter, yet love peanuts. This spread has quite a different texture and by combining raw peanuts with roasted you gain extra vitamins plus the flavour children love, without it being too salty. If the flavour of peanuts is not liked, hazelnuts or cashews can be substituted – but never send *whole* nuts in a small child's packed lunch, as they can easily be choked on.

MAKES ABOUT 1 lb (450 g)

**8 oz (225 g) roasted salt peanuts**
**8 oz (225 g) raw peanuts**
**1 tablespoon honey**
**4–6 tablespoons peanut, corn, or sunflower oil**

**1.** Rub surplus salt off roasted nuts with kitchen paper. Grind all the nuts as finely as possible in a mincer, blender or food processor. Add honey and work to a paste with sufficient oil to make an easy spreading texture.
**2.** Pack tightly into one or more screw-top jars and to maintain best flavour and food value store in refrigerator, and use within 6 weeks.
**3.** Used as a sandwich filling, peanut butter is a good alternative to meat, cheese and eggs as it is high in protein. With a little hot water stirred in to achieve a softer texture, it can be sent in a pot to eat as a dip with crisp vegetables.

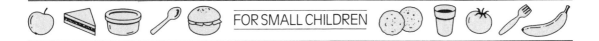

# Children's Favourite

Many small children are reluctant to eat salads, fuss about lettuce and tomatoes, and don't seem to like mayonnaise or French dressing. For all those mothers who rack their brains frantically for something their children *will* eat, try this recipe. But do remember not to mention the word 'salad'.

Use the recipe for other salads with diced turkey, beef, lamb, pork, ham, tongue, corned beef or, if preferred, cheese, nuts or hard-boiled egg.

SERVES 1

**2 tablespoons diced cooked chicken**
**1–2 tablespoons cooked peas or green beans**
**1–2 tablespoons cooked sweetcorn or baked beans**
**1 small sliced carrot, cooked or raw**
**1 tablespoon tomato ketchup**
**1 tablespoon plain yogurt**

**1.** Combine the chicken and vegetables, and mix together the ketchup and yogurt. The yogurt (which *can* be optional) reduces the strength and taste of the ketchup – makes it a prettier, less strident colour, too!
**2.** Serve in a small plastic bowl with snap-on lid, or a margarine carton. Pack a small spoon or fork with the lunch.

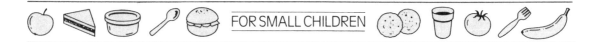
# Beef and Bacon Loaf

Ideal for a family supper, hot or cold, but also a tasty and nutritious lunch when sliced and packed into pitta bread or large baps with sliced tomato. Cut in thick slices, individually wrap in clingfilm, and freeze if wished (thaw overnight in fridge). Use within 4 days.

MAKES A 2 lb (900 g) LOAF (8–10 SLICES)

**4 oz (115 g) bacon**
**12 oz (350 g) lean minced beef**
**1 lb (450 g) beef sausagemeat**
**4 oz (115 g) wholemeal bread**
**Grated rind and juice of ½ lemon**
**½ teaspoon dried thyme**

**1.** Set oven at 180°C/350°F/Gas 4. Line base of 2 lb (1 kg) loaf tin with foil.
**2.** Mince or finely dice bacon, then combine with the beef mince and sausagemeat. Mince or process the bread into breadcrumbs, then mix breadcrumbs, lemon rind and juice and thyme into the meat.
**3.** Pack well mixed meat into loaf tin, cover tightly with foil, and set in small roasting tin half full of water. Place in the oven and bake for 1¼ hours. Cool loaf in tin and chill well before turning out.

# Orange Mousse

This pud is sugar free and chemical free, is made in a moment, and is *much* cheaper than the synthetic commercial products. Make a batch and freeze until needed (take out the night before).

MAKES 7–8

**14.5 oz (410 g) can evaporated milk**
**8.8 oz (250 ml) carton frozen concentrated orange juice**
**1 sachet gelatine**
**4 tablespoons cold water**

**1.** Chill the evaporated milk and thaw the frozen orange juice. Sprinkle gelatine on the cold water in a small pan and leave to soak and swell.
**2.** Whisk evaporated milk until thick and frothy. Warm gelatine to dissolve the crystals, but do so without boiling, then pour on to milk, whisking in thoroughly. Whisk in the orange juice, a tablespoon at a time.
**3.** Turn mousse into small lidded, fancy or plain, individual containers, and chill to set, or place in freezer.

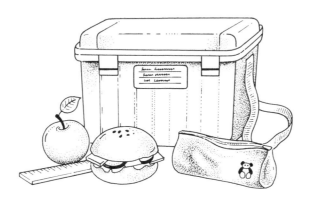

# Pineapple Jelly Cream

Very quick and easy to make from real unsweetened fruit juice, much better for children than commercial chemical jellies. Do not use the syrup from a can of pineapples as this may contain a natural enzyme that prevents gelatine setting.

Cartons of pure orange, grapefruit or mixed fruit juices can all be used to make this jelly.

SERVES 2

**½ pint (300 ml) from carton of unsweetened pineapple juice**
**1 sachet gelatine**
**5 oz (150 g) carton plain yogurt**

**1.** Place 4 tablespoons of the juice in a small pan and sprinkle on the gelatine. Leave to soak for 2–3 minutes. Warm gently without boiling until crystals have dissolved, then remove from heat.
**2.** Stir in first the remaining pineapple juice, and then the yogurt. Pour into 8 oz (225 g) margarine containers and chill overnight to set. Send in the container with a spoon. Will keep up to 4 days in the fridge.

26

# Pear Pie

Wholemeal pastry tastes delicious – especially with cinnamon added as in this pie – but it is usually very difficult to roll out. That problem is cleverly avoided here! This recipe is very popular with children for packed lunches or family desserts.

MAKES 8 SQUARES

7 oz (200 g) wholemeal flour
7 oz (200 g) plain flour
6 oz (175 g) sunflower margarine
2 teaspoons powdered cinnamon
3½ oz (100 g) soft light brown sugar
2 size 4 eggs
2 lb (900 g) ripe pears, peeled, quartered and cored

**1.** Set oven at 190°C/375°F/Gas 5. Mix flours, margarine and cinnamon together, and rub together until like breadcrumbs. Add the sugar and break in the eggs. Fork through to a rough crumbly texture without attempting to gather into a ball.
**2.** Grease an 8 × 11 inch (20 × 7.5 cm) baking or Swiss roll tin. Tip nearly two-thirds of the mixture into the tin. With floured fingers pat out mixture evenly over base and sides.
**3.** Slice the pears, arranging them over pastry in a thick layer. Cover with remaining crumbly pastry mix and press down firmly all over with floured hands. Bake for 30–35 minutes until golden, then leave to cool. Cut into eight squares (which can be individually wrapped and frozen). Transport in small polythene box, perhaps wrapped in clingfilm, and pack a spoon too.

# Chocolate and Hazelnut Loaf

A firm loaf cake that does not crumble readily, so ideal in a packed lunch. Slice thinly and sandwich two slices with butter or margarine or just serve plain. It is low in fat and high in food value, so perfect for those with small appetites.

MAKES 16–18 SLICES

**3 tablespoons warm water**
**3 tablespoons cocoa powder**
**2 × 5 oz (150 g) cartons plain yogurt**
**2 eggs**
**4 oz (115 g) soft light brown sugar**
**4 oz (115 g) chopped hazelnuts**
**6 oz (175 g) raisins**
**7 oz (200 g) wholemeal flour**
**2½ teaspoons baking powder**

**1.** Set oven at 180°C/350°F/Gas 4. Grease a 2 lb (1 kg) loaf tin and line base with greaseproof paper.
**2.** Pour warm water onto cocoa to mix to a paste, then stir in the yogurt. Add eggs, nuts and raisins, and stir very thoroughly. Shake flour and baking powder together in a bag to mix well, then fold into cake mixture.
**3.** Turn into loaf tin and bake for 1 hour or until a skewer pushed into the mixture comes out clean. Cool in tin until hand hot then turn out and cool on wire rack.

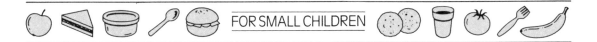

# Drinks for Schoolchildren

Many mothers find themselves faced with providing not one but two drinks every school day for their children – one for the mid-morning break, another for lunch. Most fizzy drinks provide nothing but calories and chemicals, but a careful examination of the list of contents will show that at last there are an increasing number with some worthwhile fruit content. If you have a soda syphon you can make your own adding pure fruit juices to the fizzy water instead of chemical cordials.

All commercial pure fruit juices can be mixed with extra water for a more thirst-quenching drink that is still acceptable to children, and easier on the purse strings than small cartons of fruit juice (convenient though these are).

In winter some of the following can be given hot in a Thermos:

Hot tomato juice with grated orange rind
Hot grapefruit with honey
Hot blackcurrant juice with a pinch of powdered cinnamon
Hot orange juice with a pinch of powdered ginger
Hot apple juice with a pinch of powdered cloves

Commercial milk-shake mixes and yogurt drinks are excessively sweet and synthetic tasting. Children are much better taking plain milk, unless you make your own fruit milk shakes from milk and fresh or puréed cooked fruits (and one or two spoonfuls of powdered milk for an extra creamy texture).

The traditional hot milk drinks – Ovaltine, Horlicks, etc – are still hard to beat for winter drinks, but try also carob powder from health-food shops which has a chocolate-like flavour.

# Menus for a Month

Suggestions in these weekly menu charts are for children with small appetites, particularly those of under eight to ten, who need a nutritious but not too filling or high-calorie meal. Young children are often very conservative, but with this choice you are sure to find a few combinations to suit even the fussiest.

The asterisk * marks recipes in this and other sections of the book. Check index for page numbers.

|  | Week 1 | Week 2 |
|---|---|---|
| MON | *Leek and potato soup<br>*Lamb and pea sandwich<br>Apple | Hot blackcurrant juice with cinnamon<br>*Chicken liver spread on rye bread<br>Crisp lettuce or endive |
| TUES | *Tongue and jelly sandwich<br>Tomato<br>Fruit yogurt<br>Squash | *Beef and bacon loaf<br>Cucumber and tomato salad<br>Malt bread, banana<br>Apple juice |
| WED | Celery, apple and satsuma salad<br>*Peanut butter in teacake<br>Ovaltine or Horlicks | *Lentil, celery and apple soup<br>*Crunchy bean, nut and curd sandwich<br>Pear |
| THURS | Scrambled egg sandwiches<br>Raw carrot<br>Fruit fool<br>Orange juice | Brussels sprout coleslaw<br>*Pickle and sausage sandwich<br>Apple<br>Milk |
| FRI | Hot apple juice with cloves<br>*Sultana and apricot curd sandwich<br>Shredded white cabbage | Tomato soup<br>*Cheese and cucumber roll<br>Green pepper strips<br>Raisins |

|        | Week 3 | Week 4 |
|--------|--------|--------|
| MON | *Children's favourite<br>Muesli biscuits<br>Sultanas<br>Grapefruit juice | *Cold pork and coleslaw sandwich<br>Date and honey sandwich<br>Tomato juice |
| TUES | Cucumber chunks<br>*Crunchy chocolate and banana sandwich<br>Fruit yogurt<br>Apple juice | Raw carrot<br>*American favourite sandwich<br>Banana milkshake |
| WED | Raw mange-tout peas<br>*Bacon and bean bap<br>Grapes<br>Milk | Cooked peas, potato, carrot and chicken<br>  in mayonnaise<br>*Chocolate and hazelnut loaf<br>Pineapple juice |
| THURS | Hot tomato juice with orange<br>Sticks of celery<br>*Lime and Caerphilly sandwich<br>*Pear pie | ½ corn on the cob<br>*Mortadella scone<br>*Orange mousse<br>Squash |
| FRI | Radishes<br>*Sardine and tomato sandwich<br>Plums<br>Orange juice | Watercress salad in pitta bread<br>Scotch egg<br>*Pineapple jelly cream<br>Squash |

# For Older Children and Students

Influencing older children and teenagers can be a daunting task. Obviously it will be easier to be confident that they eat a proper lunch if they have developed good eating habits at home, but parents have to be realistic. If children are sent off with dinner money in hand, they are quite likely to opt for spending it on Coke and chips daily. However confidently they assure you that they'll pick something up for lunch and save you the bother, don't be tempted – at best it will be a greasy sausage roll, or beefburger in a cotton-wool bun.

*You* know children are what they eat, that their health and looks depend on their diet, but your children will not study nutrition in school until they are about thirteen, by which time they have been influenced by a lifetime of their own bad habits, or the bad habits of their friends. Regrettably, teenagers are quite able to walk from a lesson in nutrition – in which they know they have given all the proper answers – straight to the chip shop for lunch. Because for most children of this age, nutrition seems about as relevant to their everyday lives as Greek mythology. So how can you influence them?

Firstly you do need their cooperation, but clear guidelines – like those on page 16 – are a good start. Teenage needs are obviously much greater in bulk than those of younger children, but they still must have a balanced diet with protein foods, vegetables, plus fruit, plus for many a more generous amount of the listed carbohydrate foods. These last are the cheapest, healthiest source of calories for those with large appetites.

All teenagers, boys as well as girls, become obsessed with their looks. This provides the best argument for you – and/or them – choosing a good diet. High-fibre foods, drinks free of chemicals, fresh fruit and vegetables, unprocessed food that still retains its natural fibre, vitamins, minerals and trace elements like zinc, are the best safeguard for good health and an acne-free skin. The chip shop and (sadly) most school canteens will not provide these.

Suggesting that older teenagers choose and shop for their own packed lunches will give you the chance to check what they have bought, to point out the list of contents on packets, and give general guidance. If you hand out money daily, you lose all chance of influence.

Overweight and underweight will be a problem for many. For both it is of prime importance to avoid junk food and all foods high in sugar. For the overweight choose food that requires plenty of chewing and which is low in calories – chicken drumsticks, celery, apples, brown rice, wholemeal bread (preferably crusts) – so that they can enjoy the pleasure of food in their mouths without piling on the calories. Where girls are obsessed with slimming (although possibly underweight), the ideas on page 37 should be helpful, but don't fight them by supplying obviously fattening foods – they won't eat it!

# Roly-Poly Sandwiches

There is no need to be a square when it comes to sandwiches – place the slice of fresh brown or white bread on a piece of foil or kitchen film, set fillings on top and roll up into a neat roll, securely wrapping in foil or film and then chill overnight if wished.

**Sweet-Sour liver** Spread bread generously with liver pâté, set sweet-sour pickled cucumber across bread and roll up firmly.

**Peanut butter and banana** Spread bread with plenty of peanut butter, lay small peeled whole banana on top, and roll up.

**Pickled peanut and sausage** Roll sausage meat into large fat sausages on a paper covered with chopped peanuts. Bake in moderate oven (180°C/350°F/Gas 4) until cooked, about 40 minutes. When cold wrap in bread which you have spread with pickle.

**Ham, cheese and carrot** Spread bread with curd or cream cheese. Arrange a thin layer of ham, then more cheese, roll up with raw scrubbed carrot inside.

**Egg and radish** Softly scramble an egg over a low heat with salt, pepper and ½ oz (15 g) sunflower margarine. Spread on bread while warm, lay line of radishes across sandwich and roll up.

**Cheese, celery and dates** Spread bread with cream cheese, cover with sliced celery and chopped dates and roll up firmly.

# Double Decker Sandwiches

These too are quite different from the common or garden spam butty, and are good to look at as well as eat!

**Curd, nut and carrot** Spread curd cheese on slice of bread, top with chopped hazelnuts and further slice of bread. Spread that with sunflower margarine then honey, and finish with coarsely grated carrot and more bread.

**Chicken, anchovy and tomato** Spread bread with anchovy paste or essence, and cover with sliced tomato. Top with bread, spread that with mayonnaise and sliced cooked chicken, and slap on another slice of bread.

**Bacon, cheese and cranberry** Make a sandwich of cooked cold bacon and chopped watercress. On top of that put some Cheddar cheese spread with cranberry sauce, and another slice of bread.

**Cod's roe, cucumber and capers** Place layer of cod's roe pâté on bread (if you can't find any, tuna fish will do). Sprinkle with a few capers. Cover with bread, spread that with tomato ketchup and a good layer of sliced cucumber, then top lastly with more bread.

**Ham and satsuma** Spread bottom slice of bread with a little fresh mustard or ketchup, then cover thickly with sliced ham. Top with bread and butter and sliced satsuma with more bread on top.

**Horseradish, beef and radish** Spread bread with horseradish sauce and top with cold sliced beef and bread. Spread that with mayonnaise or sunflower margarine, cover with sliced radish and top with more bread.

**Edam, ginger and apple** Sandwich two slices of bread with a good layer of Edam cheese, then top with sliced apple tossed in ginger marmalade and another layer of bread.

# Spanish Omelette 'Sandwich'

Cold omelette may come as a surprise to many, but plain, herb, cheese and ham omelettes make the quickest, most delicious fillings for crisp French bread. This recipe is for a classic Spanish omelette – which is traditionally cut in wedges and eaten like a cake accompanied by salad – but here it is cut into wedges or strips to fill rolls or French bread.

SERVES 2–4

**1 medium onion, peeled and sliced**
**8 oz (225 g) potatoes, peeled and cut in ½ inch (1.25 cm) dice**
**3 tablespoons olive oil**
**1 red or green pepper, seeded and cut into strips**
**4 eggs**
**Salt and pepper**
**1–2 teaspoons chopped fresh chives, basil or parsley**

**1.** Fry the onion and potato slowly in oil in a frying pan, approximately 9 inch (22.5 cm) in diameter. Add the pepper strips. Stir from time to time and cook until vegetables are all tender.
**2.** Whisk eggs with seasoning and herbs. Pour into pan and cook over moderate heat without stirring. When golden underneath slip pan under a hot grill to cook the upperside until set, then leave to cool. Run palette knife underneath and cut in wedges or strips. Tuck in crisp rolls or French bread, and wrap in clingfilm.

# Bacon Chowder

A substantial warming winter soup, a meal in itself. Freeze soup if you wish in handy sized portions for a later date then thaw overnight. Reheat soup at breakfast and pour into an unbreakable Thermos. Pack with a spoon and mug or vacuum flask beaker top.

MAKES 3–4 SERVINGS

5 rashers streaky bacon
1 oz (30 g) sunflower margarine
4 sticks celery, sliced
1 medium onion, peeled and chopped
1 medium potato, peeled and chopped
¾ pint (425 ml) water
1 bayleaf
4 tablespoons frozen sweetcorn kernels
½ teaspoon dried thyme
½ teaspoon salt
1 rounded tablespoon flour
1 pint (550 ml) milk

**1.** Cut rinds off rashers then snip bacon into large pieces. Fry slowly in margarine in a large saucepan until fat runs well. Add the celery, onion and potato to the pan, cooking with the bacon to lightly brown. Stir in water, bayleaf, sweetcorn, thyme and salt, then simmer for 10–15 minutes or until potato is cooked.
**2.** Mix flour with a little of the milk to make a smooth paste, then gradually work in remaining milk, keeping mixture smooth. Stir into chowder when potatoes are cooked. Bring to the boil to thicken, then discard bayleaf.

# Low-Calorie Salads for Slimmers

Many teenage girls are worried about their waistlines. Packing savoury and fruit salads will match their demands for low-calorie lunches and leave you confident they are also well nourished. Use cartons, jars or tins of unsweetened juices to make jellies, and pack crispbreads with salads.

**Savoury salads**
1. Grapefruit segments and diced pear tossed in a little honey and plenty of cottage cheese.
2. Cold diced chicken, sweetcorn, chopped pepper, combined with low-calorie salad dressing. Pack with sprigs of watercress.
3. Sliced hard-boiled egg and tomato on bed of lettuce, chopped celery and walnuts, moistened with low-calorie French dressing.

**Fruit jelly salads**
Sprinkle 1 sachet of gelatine onto 4 tablespoons fruit juice in a pan. Warm gently to melt crystals and add ¾ pint (350 ml) fruit juice, leave to cool then add prepared fresh fruit. Make two jellies using the following combinations:

Apple juice with sliced apples and grapes
Orange juice with strawberries or nectarine
Pineapple juice with banana and raisins
Grapefruit juice with honey and pear

# Bean, Bacon and Pasta Salad

A substantial salad for the ever-hungry with a large appetite. Wholemeal pasta, such as macaroni, shells or a variety of other shapes, is now also recommended to those trying to lose weight since it is satisfying to eat yet converts to calories slowly, delaying the return of hunger.

SERVES 1

1½–2 oz (40–60 g) wholemeal pasta
4 oz (115 g) green beans
2 rashers lean back bacon
2 small tomatoes
Freshly ground black pepper
1–2 tablespoons French dressing (optional)

**1.** Simmer pasta gently in very lightly salted boiling water until only just tender, not mushy. Drain and rinse under cold water. Cook green beans lightly too so that they still remain crunchy, then drain. Grill bacon until crisp, drain on kitchen paper, then chop.
**2.** Combine pasta, beans and bacon while still warm so that flavours mingle. When cold add quartered tomatoes, pepper and moisten with French dressing – or, if preferred, a few spoons of mayonnaise or yogurt.

# Crunchy Munchy Chicken Maryland

For teenagers who love to get their teeth into something, this lunch is sure to be a winner (it's equally popular hot as a supper dish). Serve with the corn, a tomato and a wholemeal roll.

SERVES 2

**2 chicken legs**
**2 tablespoons tomato ketchup**
**3–4 tablespoons rolled oats**
**½ teaspoon salt**
**1 corn on the cob**

**1.** Set oven at 200°C/400°F/Gas 6. Set chicken legs in small roasting tin lined with foil. Spread legs with ketchup and press on oats all over, sprinkle with salt and bake for 40 minutes. Spoon over juices and cook for futher 10–15 minutes or until well cooked.
**2.** Leave to cool overnight for packed lunch.
**3.** Cook corn in boiling water for 20 minutes or until a kernel will pull out easily. Cut cob in half. Sprinkle with seasoning and pack with chicken.

# Pizza Slice

Always popular, especially with young people, and excellent both warm and cold. Wrap slices individually in foil or clingfilm, and freeze if you wish. Allow two slices for good appetites.

12 SLICES

**10 oz (300 g) strong plain flour**
**½ teaspoon salt**
**1 sachet easy-blend yeast**
**2 tablespoons oil**
**⅓ pint (200 ml) warm water**
**1 large onion, peeled and chopped**
**2 tablespoons oil**
**14 oz (397 g) can tomatoes**
**1½ teaspoons dried oregano**
**Salt, pepper and sugar**
**4 oz (115 g) mushrooms, wiped and sliced**
**4 oz (115 g) ham, diced**
**5 oz (150 g) Mozzarella cheese, thinly sliced**

**1.** Mix flour, salt and yeast for pizza base, then stir in the oil and water. Work to a smooth elastic dough, then knead lightly for 2–3 minutes. Place in oiled polythene bag and leave in a warm place to double in size.
**2.** For the topping, fry onion in oil until golden, then add tomatoes and oregano. Simmer to reduce until thick and pulpy. Season with salt, pepper and sugar to taste, then cool.
**3.** Set oven at 220°C/425°F/Gas 7. Flour a large, approximately 11 × 14 inch (27.5 × 35 cm) baking tray or roasting tin. Pat or roll out dough to fit. Spread over tomato mixture, scatter with sliced mushrooms and diced ham. Cover with sliced cheese, allow to stand 10 minutes, and then bake for 17–20 minutes until golden. Cut in twelve squares and leave to cool.

# Sausage, Apple and Sage Plait

Much better than sausage rolls which are invariably very greasy, and almost all pastry with a dry centre. This plait is lovely, meaty and moist, and freezes beautifully.

SERVES 4–5

**8 oz (225 g) wholemeal flour**
**½ teaspoon salt**
**3½ oz (100 g) sunflower margarine**
**1 oz (30 g) white fat**
**4 tablespoons water**

FILLING
**1 large cooking apple, wiped, cored and finely chopped**
**2 oz (50 g) porridge oats**
**1 teaspoon fresh chopped sage**
**1 tablespoon chutney or pickle (optional)**
**1 lb (450 g) good sausagemeat**

**1.** Set oven at 200°C/400°F/Gas 6. Mix flour and salt, quickly rub in soft margarine and white fat, then stir and cut in water with a palette knife. Work to a firm dough (but not too dry or it will crack when rolling out). Roll out to an oblong approximately 11 × 14 inches (27.5 × 35 cm).
**2.** Mix all the filling ingredients together. Slip pastry onto a baking tray, lay sausagemeat in a fat roll across the entire width of pastry – parallel to the short side – and cut pastry either side of sausage into ¾ inch (1½ cm) wide ribbons at almost right angles to sausage. Starting at one end draw ribbons up and over sausage alternately one from each side to make a plait pattern. Bake for 45–60 minutes until golden.

# Old Vicarage Beef Pie

A real gem of a pie: it's easy to make, excellent hot, delectable cold, cuts like a dream without crumbling, and can be tossed in the freezer without suffering any ill effect.

SERVES 4–5

1 large onion, peeled and chopped
2 cloves of garlic, peeled and chopped
1 tablespoon oil
1 lb (450 g) best quality beef, finely minced
2 tablespoons Worcestershire sauce    2 dashes Tabasco
¼ pint (150 ml) stock, red wine or beer
1 tablespoon tomato purée
1 teaspoon sugar
1 teaspoon mixed herbs

PASTRY
8 oz (225 g) plain flour
2 oz (60 g) white fat
2 oz (60 g) sunflower margarine
½ teaspoon salt
1 egg, lightly beaten    1–2 tablespoons water

**1.** Fry onion and garlic in the oil until pale gold, then stir in the meat, frying until brown and crumbly. Add the remaining filling ingredients and cook briskly until liquid is reduced. Season to taste and cool.
**2.** Set oven at 220°C/425°F/Gas 7. Make pastry by sieving flour into bowl, then rubbing fats into flour, with the salt. Add three-quarters of the beaten egg to pastry with water, and mix to a firm dough. Roll out, and line an 8 inch (20 cm) deep pie plate with a generous half of the pastry. Pack tightly with filling, cover with remaining pastry, and brush with remaining egg. Bake for 30 minutes or until golden.

# Liver and Sausage Loaf

Delicious for a salad supper, the remainder can be used for packed lunches; or you can slice up the whole loaf when cold and freeze until required, thawing overnight. It is a good source of iron, invaluable for teenage girls. Chicken liver may be used instead of pigs' if a milder flavour is preferred.

10–12 SLICES

**2 large slices wholemeal bread**
**14 oz (400 g) pigs' liver**
**1 teaspoon dried mixed herbs**
**1 lb (450 g) good sausagemeat**
**2 tablespoons Worcestershire sauce**

**1.** Set oven at 180°C/350°F/Gas 4. Make the bread into crumbs by rubbing in the hands, or by using an electric blender or food processor. Mince the liver. If a blender is available tip out the crumbs, dice the liver and purée. If using a processor add the liver to the crumbs and work to a smooth texture. Lastly combine all ingredients and mix together thoroughly.
**2.** Turn mixture into a 2 lb (1 kg) loaf tin lined with foil at the base. Cover tightly with more foil and set in roasting tin with 1 inch (2.5 cm) water in it. Bake for 1¼ hours until firm and springy to the touch, and slightly shrunk from sides. Leave to cool in tin.

# Mushroom Flan

Perfect for those teenagers who declare they have gone vegetarian. Make in large tartlet tins – tinfoil or deep Yorkshire pudding tins are ideal – then freeze the surplus flans raw before baking freshly when required. All varieties of quiche are best if eaten within 24 hours of baking, so slip in the oven, thawed or still frozen, when cooking your evening meal. If you run short of tins, raw tarts may be knocked out when frozen, and then returned to original tin to thaw and bake later. Transport in tins for safety.

SERVES 4–5

7 oz (200 g) wholemeal flour
3½ oz (100 g) sunflower margarine
2 tablespoons water
8 oz (225 g) mushrooms, wiped and thickly sliced
1 oz (30 g) sunflower margarine
1 rounded tablespoon flour
½ pint (300 ml) milk
½ teaspoon salt
1 large egg

**1.** Set oven at 200°C/400°F/Gas 6. Make pastry by rubbing together flour and fat, then stir in water with round-ended knife to make a firm pastry. Chill well.
**2.** To make the filling, fry mushroom slices very quickly in the margarine, stirring only occasionally, until a golden brown. Remove from heat and stir in first flour then milk. Blend in very well then bring to boil to thicken. Cover and cool.
**3.** Roll out pastry to line five individual tart tins or a 7–8 inch (18–20 cm) flan tin or ring. Beat egg into mushroom sauce. Pour into pastry case. Bake for 20–30 minutes until golden and set firmly in centre.

# Chicken, Pea and Bacon Tart

Even conservative non-quiche eaters will enjoy this flan. Cut cooked in portions and freeze if wished, or make in five individual large tartlet tins, freeze raw and freshly bake the evening before they are required. Pack portion of tart in small plastic box for safe transport. Individual tartlets are best transported in the tin in which they were baked. Eat in the fingers or pack with a fork.

SERVES 4–5

1 oz (30 g) sunflower margarine
1 oz (30 g) plain flour
½ pint (300 ml) milk
4 oz (115 g) frozen peas
2 cooked chicken legs, boned and diced
1 egg   Salt and pepper
2–3 rashers of bacon, de-rinded

PASTRY
7 oz (200 g) wholemeal flour
1½ oz (40 g) white fat
2 oz (60 g) sunflower margarine
½ teaspoon salt   2½–3 tablespoons water

1. To make filling, melt margarine and stir in flour. Remove from heat, stir in milk to a smooth consistency, then bring to the boil, stirring well. Remove from heat, add peas and leave to cool. Add the chicken dice to the sauce with egg and seasoning. Stir well and leave until cold. Set oven at 200°C/400°F/Gas 6.
2. To make the pastry, put flour in a bowl, and rub both fats into flour. Add salt then mix in water to make a firm dough. Roll out to line an 8 inch (20 cm) flan ring or flan tin (or smaller individual tins). Fill with chicken and pea mixture. Snip bacon into small pieces. Scatter all over top of flan. Bake for 40 minutes or until golden and crispy on top and sauce filling is set in centre.

# Blackberry and Apple Mousse

Inspired by this lovely light mousse, perhaps you can persuade the family to go blackberrying at the weekends in the autumn so you can make this recipe again. It freezes well.

SERVES 6–8

12 oz (350 g) cooking apples, peeled, cored and sliced
6 oz (175 g) blackberries
6 tablespoons water
1 sachet gelatine
3 large eggs, separated
4 oz (115 g) caster sugar
¼ pint (150 ml) plain yogurt

1. Cook apples with blackberries in half the water until pulpy. Place remaining water in a cup, and sprinkle on gelatine. As soon as the fruit is cooked, stir in the soaked gelatine then purée finely. Whisk egg whites to a snow and then whisk in 1 tablespoon of sugar. Whisk remaining sugar with warm fruit purée and egg yolks, to a thick light mousse.
2. Combine the fruit and egg white mixtures in whichever bowl is biggest, add yogurt, and fold together carefully. Turn into 6–8 individual cartons and chill to set.

# Pear and Cinnamon Crumble

This easy dessert – that freezes well – can be made with any stewed or puréed fruits that have been cooked with very little liquid – plums, apricots, gooseberries, blackberries and apples. You could also have a bag of ready-made topping in the freezer – a marvellous way of using up bread that is past its prime for sandwiches.

MAKES 6–8

**1½ lb (675 g) pears, peeled, quartered and cored**
**6 tablespoons water**
**6 oz (175 g) wholemeal breadcrumbs**
**3 oz (90 g) sunflower margarine**
**3 tablespoons demerara sugar**
**1 teaspoon powdered cinnamon**

**1.** Set oven at 190°C/375°F/Gas 5. Roughly chop pears and stew gently in a covered pan with water until just soft. Allow to cool.
**2.** Sprinkle breadcrumbs into a roasting tin, dot with margarine and sprinkle with sugar. Bake until crisp and golden, about 15–20 minutes, giving the occasional stir so that the crumbs round the edge of the tin do not become too brown. Leave to cool, then stir in cinnamon.
**3.** To complete, divide pears between 6–8 cartons (old small margarine tubs are ideal) and top with crumbs. Cover tops firmly with foil or thick film for absolute security.

# Date and Banana Bread

Over-ripe bananas can often be found in the bargain basket at greengrocers. Most teenagers would turn their noses up at them, but they make a delicious and beautifully moist bread. Do not cut too thin.

10–12 SLICES

**1 lb (450 g) over-ripe bananas, peeled and mashed**
**4 oz (115 g) dates, chopped**
**Grated rind and juice of 1 small lemon**
**4 oz (115 g) sunflower margarine**
**2 oz (50 g) soft light brown sugar**
**2 eggs**
**6 oz (175 g) wholemeal flour**
**1½ teaspoons baking powder**

**1.** Set oven at 180°C/350°F/Gas 4. Grease a 2 lb (1 kg) loaf tin and line base with greaseproof paper. Mix the mashed bananas with the chopped dates, mashing them together. Add grated rind and juice of lemon, the margarine, sugar and eggs. Beat together well to mix thoroughly.
**2.** Shake flour and baking powder in a bag to mix the raising agent evenly. Fold into the cake mixture and turn into loaf tin. Bake for 1–1¼ hours until a skewer inserted into the centre comes out clean. Leave in tin until hand hot, then turn onto a wire rack to finish cooling.

# Pineapple and Sultana Cake

Easy enough for teenagers to make themselves. It's delicious warm from the oven as a pud served with plain yogurt, and you will have to hide the rest for packed lunches. Or better still make two! Cut in slices and individually wrap in clingfilm to freeze until required. Very moist cake does not require spreading with butter but for the ever-hungry, sandwich two slices with cream or curd cheese, preferably while still frozen so it will not crumble.

3½ oz (100 g) sunflower margarine
3½ oz (100 g) soft brown sugar
1 size 1 egg
3½ oz (100 g) sultanas
12 oz (340 g) can crushed pineapple in syrup
9 oz (250 g) wholemeal flour
2 level teaspoons baking powder

**1.** Set oven at 180°C/350°F/Gas 4. Grease a 2 lb (1 kg) loaf tin, and line base with foil or greaseproof paper. Stir together margarine, sugar, egg, sultanas and pineapple. Combine wholemeal flour and baking powder by shaking together in polythene bag so they are evenly mixed (they cannot be sifted together as when a white flour is used, unless a very coarse sieve is available).
**2.** Fold flour into pineapple mixture and turn into prepared tin. Bake for 1¼ hours or until a fine skewer pushed into the centre comes out clean. Leave in tin until hand hot, then turn out onto wire rack to cool completely. Slice when cold.

# Menus for a Month

The asterisks *, as before, mark recipes in this and other sections, many of which can be prepared for family meals or the freezer to simplify the making of packed lunches. The fourth-week menus are for weight-watchers. Bread, not crisps, chocolate or biscuits, is the healthiest filler for the ever-hungry. Choose a good variety to maintain interest and ensure it is very fresh, or at least fresh from the freezer. Stale bread makes packed lunches very dreary.

| | **Week 1** | **Week 2** |
|---|---|---|
| MON | *Leek and potato soup<br>*Pizza slices<br>Banana | *Horseradish, beef and radish sandwich<br>Raw cauliflower<br>*Pear pie<br>Milk |
| TUES | *Chicken, pea and bacon tart<br>Raw carrots<br>*Lemon and walnut sandwich<br>Orange juice | *Lentil, celery and apple soup<br>*Curd, nut and carrot double decker<br>Plums |
| WED | *Crunchy munchy chicken Maryland<br>Sweetcorn and tomato salad<br>*Pineapple and sultana cake<br>Milk | *Bacon, cheese and cranberry double decker<br>Apple crumble<br>Pineapple juice |
| THURS | *Old Vicarage beef pie<br>Watercress and satsuma salad<br>*Date and banana bread<br>Tomato juice | *Tuna, cucumber and caper sandwich<br>Tomatoes<br>Fruit yogurt |
| FRI | *Spanish omelette in French bread<br>Lettuce<br>*Pear and cinnamon crumble<br>Apple juice | Tomato soup<br>*Sausage, apple and sage plait<br>Grapes, celery and cucumber |

|  | **Week 3** | **Week 4** |
|---|---|---|
| MON | *Bacon chowder<br>*Edam, ginger and apple double decker<br>Orange juice | *Chicken, sweetcorn and pepper savoury<br>   salad<br>*Pineapple, banana and raisin jelly<br>Skimmed milk |
| TUES | *Mushroom flan<br>Tomato salad<br>Satsuma<br>Milk | *Grapefruit, pear, and cottage cheese<br>   savoury salad<br>*Apple and grape jelly<br>Tomato juice |
| WED | *Sweet-sour liver roly-poly sandwiches<br>*Pineapple and sultana cake<br>Banana milk shake | *Egg, tomato, watercress, celery and<br>   walnut savoury salad<br>Wholemeal pitta bread<br>*Orange and nectarine jelly<br>Lime juice |
| THURS | *Ham, cheese and carrot roly-poly<br>   sandwiches<br>*Plum crumble (see Pear crumble)<br>Blackcurrant juice | *Wholemeal spinach flan, and cucumber<br>*Pineapple jelly cream<br>Orange juice |
| FRI | Grapefruit juice<br>*Egg and radish roly-poly sandwich<br>*Chocolate and hazelnut loaf | *Liver and sausage loaf on crispbreads<br>*Blackberry and apple mousse<br>Mixed citrus juice |

# Desk-Top Dining

Beat the tax on take-aways and take your own. Avoid those greasy canteen lunches and junk foods at the local snack bar, and eat in style at your desk. Whether you are a high-fibre fanatic (eating beans and bran and wholemeal everything) or are following the more recent slow-conversion seekers (lots of pasta and rice) for that long-lasting full feeling – or just plain hungry at lunchtime – the following recipes for desk-top dining will provide you with the opportunity to stick to a healthy diet a little more often.

The conditions attached to packed lunches for smaller and older children apply equally here as well. The lunch should be well balanced, with the right combination of protein, carbohydrate, fruit and vegetables, but the high-calorie foods should be watched, particularly if the desk-sitting is not tempered with exercise. Low animal-fat diets are recommended for everybody, so choose low-fat proteins – low-fat cheeses, say, to replace, *not* as well as, meat, fish or eggs. Pick low-cholesterol margarines like sunflower, and avoid bought pies and pastries (select fats carefully if you make your own). To keep sugar intake low, take plenty of fresh fruit daily, and treat yourself to a wide variety of these as they come into season.

Do spare a thought for your business colleagues when desk-top dining. The office in the middle of the day provides neither the time nor the place to indulge a passion for garlic, raw onions, curry or kippers! Dispose of citrus peel in a sealed bag, and wash your hands before you spread a lingering aroma all around you.

# Pitta Pockets

Use these sophisticated combinations for filling pitta breads or sandwiches or for making salads. Either cut pittas in half lengthwise, or cut a narrow sliver off the long side and open up to fill.

**Italian** Spread inside with anchovy paste or essence. Fill with sliced hard-boiled egg and thickly sliced tomatoes tossed in seasoning, a little olive oil and chopped marjoram or basil. Add a few stoned black olives.

**Hongroise** Mix curd cheese with paprika and tomato purée to taste. Spread pitta breads inside liberally with this and fill with sliced raw mushroom and crisp lettuce.

**Majorcan** Spread bread with good mayonnaise and fill with sliced chicken, segments of orange, crisp lettuce and diced red pepper or pimento.

**Normande** Spread with cream cheese and fill with crisp apple slices (dipped in salted water to prevent browning), sliced celery and walnut pieces.

**Niçoise** Flake tinned tuna and a little of its oily juices with salt and pepper. Spread inside pitta bread and fill with crisp lettuce, sliced cucumber and tomato.

**Indienne** Spread with curry-flavoured mayonnaise, fill with sliced chicken, seeded or seedless green grapes, stoned ripe apricots and watercress.

**Flamande** Spread with mustard, fill with sliced beef, finely shredded red cabbage or pickled cabbage and chopped capers.

**Oriental** Spread with pear yogurt with sliced banana tossed in and fill with sliced cucumber and chicken dusted with a little ground ginger.

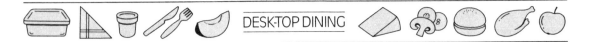

# Kidney and Sherry Soup

A delicious and warming soup, as welcome in a heated office as on an outdoor moveable feast on a cold winter's day.

SERVES 6

8 oz (225 g) beef kidney
2 tablespoons oil
1 medium carrot, peeled and diced
1 medium onion, peeled and diced
2 sticks celery, trimmed and sliced
2 pints (a good litre) chicken stock
2 tablespoons tomato purée
1 bouquet garni
1 tablespoon sunflower margarine
1 tablespoon flour
2 glasses sherry

**1.** Remove core of kidney and cut in thin slices. Fry in oil in a saucepan very quickly. Add the vegetables to the pan and brown these also for 3–4 minutes. Pour on stock, add tomato purée and bouquet garni (bunch of fresh or dried herbs), cover and simmer for 40 minutes.
**2.** Mix margarine and flour to a paste, and remove bouquet garni from soup. Stir in paste, bring to the boil, then cool soup a little before puréeing until smooth. Season to taste and freeze if wished when cold. Reheat soup, add the sherry and pour into Thermos.

# Artichoke with Broad Beans and Bacon Dip

For the jaded desk-top diner who really wants something impressive and a bit different. Remember to pack a bag for the leaves as they are discarded. Vegetarians can omit the bacon or replace it with a little cottage cheese.

SERVES 1

**1 plump globe artichoke**
**4 oz (115 g) broad beans, fresh or frozen**
**2 rashers bacon**
**1 oz (30 g) sunflower margarine**
**1 teaspoon lemon juice**
**Salt and pepper**

**1.** Trim stalk off artichoke and cook in large pan of boiling salted water, stalk end uppermost, for 30–40 minutes. The leaves will pull out easily when cooked. Drain and rinse under cold running water briefly and leave to cool.

**2.** Cook broad beans in boiling salted water until they are tender. Meanwhile grill bacon until crisp. Drain beans, reserving 3–4 tablespoons of their cooking liquid. Purée beans using a food processor, blender or vegetable mouli, adding margarine and lemon juice with enough liquid to make a soft purée. Stir in roughly chopped bacon, season to taste, and chill overnight.

**3.** Ease back the leaves from the centre of the artichoke when cold, to reveal the choke – the thistle-like centre. Scrape out the thready choke with a teaspoon leaving the fleshy base. The dip may be used to fill the artichoke centre or can be packed separately. A teaspoon or fork may be useful for eating the heart.

# Smoked Mackerel
# and Horseradish Pâté

This pâté can be used as a sandwich filling or served with salads. Excellent but more expensive made with smoked trout, you will need to buy about 1 lb (450 g) to allow for additional weight of head and bones. A horseradish-flavoured quark is available in some shops and could be used for this recipe. Freeze if wished. Slimmers can omit the margarine.

SERVES 4–5

**12 oz (350 g) smoked mackerel**
**8 oz (225 g) quark or cottage cheese**
**3 teaspoons horseradish sauce**
**Juice of ½ lemon**
**3½ oz (100 g) sunflower margarine**

**1.** Rip skin off mackerel and carefully check to remove all bones. Pound all ingredients together thoroughly by hand, or purée finely in a food processor.
**2.** If using an electric blender, warm margarine to just melt it, and pour into blender goblet. Add lemon juice and fish first then, when smooth, tip in the horseradish and cheese so that the pâté will turn more easily on the blades.
**3.** Turn into 4–6 handy-sized containers and freeze some for a later date.

# Lentil Spread

This is a delicious pâté. If you prefer, make it with continental lentils, and double the water used and the cooking time. Yeast extract can be replaced with chopped mint to give a very different flavour, especially useful for vegetarians who might be taking lentil sandwiches regularly for lunch.

Lentils are very high in food value, and are one of the three most popular pulses in Europe.

**4 oz (115 g) split lentils**
**7 oz (200 g) water**
**4 tablespoons oil**
**1 teaspoon yeast extract**

**1.** Place lentils and water together in a pan and simmer gently for 15 minutes until soft. Leave covered in pan to cool, then purée finely with oil and yeast extract. The split lentils will make a smooth pâté, the continental lentils will make a rougher textured spread.
**2.** Store in screw-topped jar for up to 4 days in the fridge.

# Lentil and Brown Rice Salad

Brown rice and lentils take some time to cook, but both may be cooked in bulk and frozen in advance. Soaking pulses overnight can cut cooking times by more than half. Follow this by thorough rinsing to remove a type of sugar which causes indigestion.

SERVES 2

**2 oz (60 g) brown or continental lentils**
**Chicken stock or water**
**2 oz (60 g) brown rice**
**1 small green pepper, diced**
**1 oz (30 g) chopped walnuts**
**¼ cucumber, diced**
**2 sticks celery, trimmed and sliced**
**2 oz (60 g) button mushrooms, wiped and sliced**

DRESSING
**½ teaspoon Dijon mustard**
**1 teaspoon honey**
**2 teaspoons wine vinegar**
**2 tablespoons olive oil**
**1 teaspoon chopped fresh savory or parsley**

**1.** Soak lentils overnight in cold water. Rinse very thoroughly in a colander and cook in unsalted chicken stock or water. Boil rapidly for 10 minutes then simmer for 20 minutes or until tender. Drain and rinse. Meanwhile, cook rice in boiling salted water separately for 45 minutes and drain.

**2.** Drop pepper dice in boiling salted water for 2 minutes to blanch and make more digestible. Cool and mix with walnuts and other vegetables. Mix vegetables with brown rice and lentils. Combine ingredients for dressing, toss all together, and season to taste.

# Tabooli

Leave your wheat to soak while you get dressed or have breakfast, or prepare the day before if you prefer. Tabooli is delicious with chopped spring onions added, but these are rather anti-social for desk-top dining, so have been omitted and peas added instead.

SERVES 2

**Chicken stock or water**
**4 oz (115 g) bulgar wheat**
**½ cucumber**
**3 tomatoes**
**1 tablespoon chopped mint or mint sauce**
**Grated rind and juice of ½ lemon**
**3 tablespoons olive oil**
**4 tablespoons cooked peas**
**Salt and black pepper**

**1.** Pour warm stock or water on wheat and leave to soak for 20 minutes. Dice cucumber and tomatoes. Combine mint, lemon and oil to make a dressing.
**2.** Drain wheat in a fine sieve pressing well to extract surplus moisture or tip onto a cloth and wring out surplus firmly. Combine wheat, diced vegetables, peas and dressing, and toss well together, seasoning to taste.
**3.** Pack in a lidded plastic container, and use a spoon to eat.

# Cumberland Celery
# and Crisp Apple Salad

A crisp and juicy salad perfect with pork, ham or tongue, cold turkey or pork pie. Do not toss salad together until just ready to serve, otherwise juices will be drawn from the orange and make the dressing puddly and thin.

SERVES 2

**1 tablespoon redcurrant jelly**
**2 teaspoons wine vinegar**
**1 tablespoon salad oil**
**¼ teaspoon salt**
**Pinch of Cayenne**
**1 large orange**
**1 Granny Smith apple**
**2 sticks celery, trimmed and sliced**

**1.** Beat jelly until smooth then gradually beat in vinegar and oil then season with salt and Cayenne. Grate rind of ½ orange and add to dressing.
**2.** Wipe, quarter and core apple, then thickly slice and toss well in dressing to prevent browning. Turn into chosen container for serving salad. Arrange layer of sliced celery on top. Peel orange then either cut into segments or halve and cut across in slices. Arrange on top of the celery. Cover and chill. To serve toss all together well.

# Steak Salad with Horseradish Cream

A colourful salad which will please both the conventional and those with more sophisticated tastes. Use lemon juice not vinegar in dressing, or peas or beans will discolour.

SERVES 2

**10 oz (275 g) thick slice best rump steak**
**4 tablespoons salad oil**
**¼ glass red wine**
**Freshly ground black pepper**
**7 oz (200 g) mange-tout peas or French beans**
**3 tomatoes**
**1 tablespoon lemon juice**
**2 teaspoons horseradish sauce**
**2 teaspoons Dijon mustard**
**3 tablespoons plain yogurt**

**1.** Marinate steak in 2 tablespoons oil, the wine and pepper, preferably overnight. Turn occasionally. Grill or fry very quickly until well browned on both sides, but medium rare. Leave to cool. Simmer peas or beans in boiling salted water to very lightly cook. Drain and cool. Scald tomatoes in boiling water for 7–8 seconds, plunge in cold water, then peel and quarter.
**2.** Make French dressing with remaining oil, lemon juice and half the horseradish and mustard. Season to taste. Cut steak into small finger size pieces and toss with peas or beans, tomatoes and French dressing. Flavour yogurt with remaining horseradish and mustard. Pack salad in lidded carton and top with a dollop of horseradish dressing.

# Tarragon and Chicken Coleslaw

Make up the delicious tarragon dressing and store in the fridge for up to 3 weeks, or deep freeze if wished. There will be enough for three or four salads. Use raw Brussels sprouts to replace white cabbage when these are in season if wished: they have a good nutty flavour. A lovely salad for weight watchers.

SERVES 1

**1 cooked chicken joint**
**3½ oz (100 g) white cabbage, finely shredded**
**1 medium carrot, peeled and coarsely grated**
**3 tablespoons canned or fresh chopped pineapple, drained**
**1 tablespoon plain yogurt**
**2 tablespoons tarragon dressing (see below)**
**Salt and pepper**

DRESSING

**3 tablespoons tarragon vinegar**
**1 tablespoon castor sugar**
**1 size 1 egg**

**1.** To make the dressing, place vinegar, sugar and egg in a small bowl and whisk well to mix. Set bowl in roasting tin of simmering water on cooker and stir with a wooden spoon until mixture thickens like a lemon curd. Tip into a screw-top jam jar, store in fridge, and use as required.
**2.** Cut chicken into fingers off the bone, and toss with remaining ingredients. Flavour with tarragon dressing and season lightly with salt and pepper to taste. Turn into a carton (a 1 lb or 450 g margarine carton is ideal), and it may be chilled overnight. Serve with a wholemeal roll if wished.

# Lime Barbecued Chicken

With a lovely fresh spring flavour, this chicken is delicious with a salad of cooked baby new potatoes, peas and raw diced cucumber tossed in a little mint. If available use raw mange-touts instead of peas.

SERVES 1

**1 tablespoon lime marmalade**
**1 teaspoon Worcestershire sauce**
**Pinch of Cayenne**
**Salt and pepper**
**1 chicken joint**

**1.** Combine the barbecue dressing of lime marmalade, Worcestershire sauce, Cayenne and a little salt and pepper. Allow chicken joint to marinate in this for at least 1 hour, if possible overnight, in an ovenproof dish.
**2.** Heat oven to 190°C/375°F/Gas 5. Bake the chicken for 40–50 minutes, basting with the juices once during cooking. The chicken is cooked when juices run clear when joint is pierced at the thickest part. Baste with any juices in dish and leave to cool.
**3.** Pack in carton or wrap in foil, and take a salad in a separate lidded container.

# Hot Pepper Casserole

While soups are one way of packing a hot course for a portable meal when weather is really cold, a hot main course instead is also most welcome. Rice, pasta and potatoes do not keep hot well, so pack bread to accompany. Green vegetables should be avoided, but all the beans and lentils plus root vegetables apart from potatoes withstand keeping hot.

SERVES 4–5

3 oz (90 g) haricot or kidney beans, soaked
1½ lb (675 g) stewing steak, cut in large cubes
1 tablespoon oil
2 onions, peeled and diced
1 red pepper, seeded and diced
3 teaspoons mild paprika
1 tablespoon flour
¾ pint (425 ml) chicken stock (but see method)
8 oz (225 g) smoked sausage, sliced
8 oz (225 g) sweetcorn kernels

**1.** Soak beans overnight, by pouring on boiling water. Fry beef in very hot oil until golden. Add onion and pepper dice to the pan and cook until beginning to soften (about 10 minutes). Stir in paprika and flour, and cook for 1 minute.

**2.** Drain beans and rinse well under running water to make more digestible, then add to pan with stock. (If only stock cube is available add water only. Add the stock cube when beans are tender to prevent salt toughening skins.) Cover and cook for 1½–2 hours until tender. Add sausage slices with sweetcorn to casserole. Season to taste. Freeze in portions if wished then reheat and turn into wide-necked Thermos.

**3.** Pack with a fork or spoon and serve in Thermos top or in a plastic bowl.

# Wholemeal Spinach Flan

Ideal for the high-fibre conscious or for vegetarians. Serve with a salad of tomatoes and raw mushrooms with a lemony French dressing. Bake in individual tins, if preferred. These can be frozen before cooking, and baked the evening before needed.

SERVES 4

**7 oz (200 g) wholemeal flour**
**Pinch of salt**
**3 oz (90 g) sunflower margarine**
**1 oz (30 g) low-cholesterol white fat**
**2 tablespoons water**

FILLING
**1 lb (450 g) frozen spinach, thawed**
**⅓ pint (200 ml) milk**
**4 tablespoons dried milk    2 eggs**
**Large pinch of nutmeg**
**½ teaspoon salt**
**Freshly ground black pepper**
**2 tablespoons grated Parmesan cheese**

**1.** Set oven at 190°C/375°F/Gas 5. Prepare pastry by putting flour and salt into bowl and rubbing fats into it. Stir water in with a blunt-ended knife, until a dough is formed. Chill.
**2.** Meanwhile prepare filling. If frozen puréed spinach is used, simply beat in remaining filling ingredients. If frozen leaf spinach, purée in food processor or electric blender.
**3.** Roll out pastry and use to line an 8 inch (20 cm) flan ring or metal flan tin, or 6 deep Yorkshire pudding tins. Pour in spinach filling, sprinkle with cheese, and bake 20–30 minutes or until filling has set in centre.

# Hi-Fi Fruit Loaf

Just the loaf for health-conscious weight-watchers who have a weakness for cakes and like a little treat now and then. This loaf is made without fat or sugar, is high in natural fibre, and is beautifully moist and mouth-wateringly fruity.

12–14 SLICES

**4 oz (115 g) dried apricots**
**8 oz (225 g) dates**
**½ pint (300 ml) orange juice**
**Grated rind and juice of ½ lemon**
**1 egg**
**2 oz (60 g) unblanched almonds, roughly chopped**
**4 oz (115 g) All-Bran**
**6 oz (175 g) wholemeal flour**
**3 teaspoons baking powder**

**1.** Soak apricots overnight or buy 'moisturised' dried apricots. Set oven at 180°C/350°F/Gas 4. Grease a 2 lb (1 kg) loaf tin and line base with greaseproof paper.
**2.** Chop dates and apricots, and place in saucepan with orange juice. Bring to the boil and simmer for 2–3 minutes. Crush with a potato masher to reduce dates to a pulp then leave to cool.
**3.** When fruit mixture is cold, stir in lemon rind and juice, egg, almonds, All-Bran and, lastly, the wholemeal flour evenly combined with the baking powder. Fold all together and turn into prepared tin. Bake for 50–60 minutes. Test with a fine skewer which should come out clean. Freeze if wished, cutting in slices first for convenience, and wrapping individually.

# Apple, Pear and Vine Salad

A fruit salad is always most refreshing, and you can use pure breakfast fruit juices to make a variety of fresh and dried fruit salads. Leave skin on fruit, if possible, to keep your salad high in fibre.

SERVES 2

**1 Cox's apple**
**1 ripe pear**
**1 tablespoon lemon juice**
**6 tablespoons pure orange juice**
**4 oz (115 g) green grapes or black grapes**
**4 ripe plums**
**4 tablespoons seeded raisins**
**2 tablespoons walnut pieces**

**1.** Wipe apple and pear, quarter, core and thickly slice. Toss in lemon juice then add orange juice. Wash and halve grapes and plums, and discard seeds and stones. Add to first fruits with raisins and nuts.
**2.** Turn into water-tight plastic container or jar. Chill overnight if made in advance. Pack with a spoon.

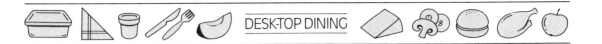

# Menus for a Month

As always, the asterisk * marks recipes which appear in various sections throughout the book (refer to the index). The four weekly menus are different and healthy, but for variety and to suit different tastes and needs, Week 3 is vegetarian and Week 4 is low-cholesterol.

| | **Week 1** | **Week 2** |
|---|---|---|
| MON | Tomato juice<br>*Tarragon and chicken coleslaw<br>Rye bread<br>Banana | Grapefruit juice<br>Cold pork<br>*Cumberland celery and crisp apple salad<br>*Pineapple and sultana cake |
| TUES | *Kidney and sherry soup<br>Celery, orange and cottage cheese salad<br>Wholemeal roll<br>Pear | Raw mushroom salad<br>*Flamande pitta pocket<br>*Apple crumble (see Pear crumble) |
| WED | *Indienne pitta pocket<br>Green salad and French dressing<br>*Orange mousse | *Lime barbecued chicken with potato, cucumber and mange-tout salad and mint French dressing<br>Grapes |
| THURS | *Steak salad with horseradish cream<br>*Date and banana bread<br>Sharon fruit | *Leek and potato soup<br>*Majorcan sandwich<br>Melon |
| FRI | Orange juice<br>*Italian sandwich<br>*Apple, pear and vine salad | *Hot pepper casserole<br>French bread<br>*Orange and nectarine jelly |

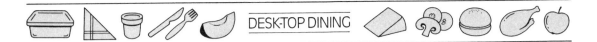
|        | Week 3 | Week 4 |
|--------|--------|--------|
| MON | *Tabooli<br>Cottage cheese with fresh or frozen raspberries<br>*Chocolate and hazelnut loaf | Watercress and beansprout salad<br>*Oriental pitta pockets<br>Kiwi fruit |
| TUES | Carrot salad<br>*Hongroise sandwich<br>*Pear and cinnamon crumble | *Lentil, celery and apple soup<br>*Smoked mackerel and horseradish pâté<br>Wholemeal roll<br>Slices of fresh pineapple |
| WED | Avocado<br>*Wholemeal spinach flan<br>Tomato salad<br>Dates | Grapefruit<br>*Artichoke with broad bean and bacon dip<br>*Hi-fi fruit loaf |
| THURS | Tomato juice<br>*Leek and Lymeswold salad<br>*Lemon and walnut sandwich | Fennel salad<br>*Niçoise sandwich<br>*Grapefruit, honey and pear jelly |
| FRI | Orange juice<br>*Lentil and brown rice salad<br>*Blackberry and apple mousse | *Pizza slice<br>Tomato and satsuma salad<br>Strawberries with plain yogurt |

# Picnics

The first picnics in Britain were enjoyed in about the middle of the eighteenth century, and they were very different in essence from those of today. For at these picnics, all the individuals present had to contribute some food or drink to the meal. It was this feature that was the most important – the combined contribution – not the eating outside which is such an essential part of the occasion today. It seems a pity that this aspect has been lost, for a shared responsibility can increase the enjoyment for all.

However a picnic can still be the most relaxed and enjoyable of meals, whether eaten in the summer on the beach or in a field, or in the winter from the boot of a car at a point-to-point. A little planning, the right equipment and food to suit the occasion and venue, and each picnic will be a joy to remember.

And never forget the impromptu picnic, where you buy everything at the other end. Some of the most memorable and delightful picnics are those when travelling, when you take advantage of the 'fat of the land'. Whether it is stalls laden with luscious fruit in a French market, a fragrant continental bakery or charcuterie, or the freshly baked pasties and splits, plus cider and clotted cream of the West Country – with a few basic essentials on hand you can enjoy a truly spontaneous and delicious picnic. Always make sure the shops will be open when you wish to buy, and prepare yourself with the following 'ingredients' for success: corkscrew/bottle opener; can opener; small serrated knife; damp J-cloth; paper table napkins; clear plastic beakers (not paper, for wine!); bag for rubbish; paper plates and plastic cutlery (optional); tea towel to use as a tablecloth; container of water (for washing fruit and sticky fingers).

# Family Picnics

Picnics can provide some of the happiest family memories and only need a minimum of preparation for complete success. Never forget to plan food and drink according to likes, dislikes, age-group, mode of travel, weight and weather – and the following tips will be useful. And do cross-refer to the other sections for more food ideas.

**Lightweight Picnics** If travelling by public transport, hiking or biking, a light picnic is all important. Insulated picnic bags or a good rucksack may be more useful than the cumbersome rigid insulated picnic boxes. Drinks are always the heaviest part of any picnic, so plan to buy them at your destination; if confident of finding drinking water, take just juice concentrate. Hikers and bikers need particularly lightweight high-energy foods: fruit and nut bars, dried fruit, gingerbread, cheese, or many recipes in the packed lunch section will be useful. Plenty of good crisp juicy apples will freshen the mouth.

**Car Trips** As soon as the family get in the car the first thought will be 'When will we stop for lunch?', so do not pack all the food in the boot. Children over six may welcome individual screw-topped bottles filled with fruit drinks, so that they can take a swig whenever they want. (Have some mugs with spouts for younger ones.) Non-messy fresh fruit such as apples, bananas and small bags of dried fruits make good nibbles to keep everyone going. Recipes and ideas in the packed lunch sections will be useful, too.

**Beach Picnics** Hand out drinks first, as not everyone will manage to juggle food and drink simultaneously. Avoid having to prepare food on the beach, but a small sharp knife is useful to quarter fruit and tomatoes and cut cake. A Thermos of hot soup or milk drink is very welcome to those who bravely swim in British coastal waters!

Sand-free sandwiches is the main aim, so choose secure fillings – cream not grated cheese, large slices of meat, not little bits of salad which will drop in the sand. Avoid hard-boiled eggs: whole, they roll off a plate; halved, the yolks will fall out. See other sections for suitable sandwiches. A large box of salad items from which foods may be selected one at a time to eat in the fingers is ideal, with items such as chicken drumsticks, cold sausages, slices of Spanish omelette or pie, sticks of cheese, carrot, celery and cucumber, tomatoes, radishes and small leaves of crisp lettuce. Do keep items small, as you will be annoyed if large items are dropped and wasted. Offer more drinks again before getting out the fruit, dessert or cake.

**Barbecue Picnics** These are always tremendous fun, and are an essential ingredient of picnics in Australia. There are many portable barbecues (leave plenty of time for them to cool down, though, before packing away). Select the site of a camp-fire with great care, and always make sure that you *can* light a fire there, and that it is completely out and dead before you leave.

# Lentil, Celery and Apple Soup

A delicious soup for a cool-weather picnic, or after a bracing swim – and it's very easy to make. It freezes beautifully if you want to stock up the freezer before the holidays. If you have cooked your own ham or bacon joint the unused cooking liquid is delicious for this soup (if too salty dilute with water before use). If ham stock is not available use water and two chicken stock cubes.

SERVES 5–6

**5 sticks celery, washed and sliced**
**8 oz (225 g) split (red) lentils**
**2 pints (a good 1 litre) ham stock**
**Pinch of ground cloves**
**1–2 Cox or Sturmer apples, quartered, cored and finely chopped**

**1.** Place celery in pan with lentils and stock. Simmer for 20–25 minutes until lentils are soft. Purée or mash until smooth.
**2.** Reheat soup with cloves and apple, and dilute with a little extra water or stock if too thick. Season to taste.

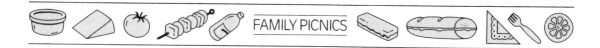
# Salmon and Dill Mousse

Quick and easy to make, you should use pink, not the more expensive red, salmon.

SERVES 4–5

8 oz (220 g) can pink salmon
¼ pint (150 ml) good mayonnaise
2 tablespoons tomato purée
1 sachet gelatine
3 tablespoons water
5 oz (150 g) carton plain yogurt
1 teaspoon dried dill

**1.** Mash entire contents of tin of salmon to a very fine purée (or mix in electric blender or food processor) with mayonnaise and then beat in tomato purée.
**2.** Sprinkle gelatine on water in pan. Leave to soak for 1 minute then heat gently to melt crystals. Fold together salmon, yogurt, dill and gelatine, season to taste, then turn into small dish or container. Chill until set.

# Stuffed Picnic Loaf

It looks like a plain loaf but when you slice this up for the family they are in for quite a surprise. Choose a thick French loaf known in France as a baguette: it's about 18 inches (45 cm) long.

SERVES 6

**4 hard-boiled eggs**
**8 oz (225 g) low-fat soft cheese**
**1 teaspoon dried parsley**
**½ teaspoon dried mixed herbs**
**8 oz (225 g) ham, finely diced**
**3½ oz (100 g) cooked peas**
**Salt and pepper**
**8 oz (225 g) long crusty loaf**

**1.** Peel and lightly mash the eggs, then beat into the cheese with the parsley and mixed herbs. Fold in the ham and peas, and season to taste.
**2.** With a bread knife, cut down the side of the bread and split it along its whole length. Open wide, and remove some of the soft crumbs from the centre of the loaf. Pack in the prepared filling, then fold back the top to reshape the loaf and hide the filling. Wrap firmly in kitchen film or foil and chill for 1–2 hours or overnight.

# Savoury Scone

Moist and light, this scone is ideal for a vegetarian picnic or as an accompaniment for cold meats. Make with wholemeal flour if you prefer.

It's at its best freshly baked, so prepare the vegetables well in advance, adding all but the flour and raising agent, then pop the finished scone in the oven while you pack the rest of the picnic. Transport in tin covered with foil.

16 FINGERS

1 medium onion, peeled and chopped
1 red pepper, seeded and chopped
3½ oz (100 g) butter or sunflower margarine
3 oz (90 g) peas (or courgettes, finely diced)
4 oz (115 g) Cheddar cheese, coarsely grated
1 tablespoon dried parsley
1 teaspoon dried mixed herbs
Salt and pepper
5 oz (150 g) carton plain yogurt
8 oz (225 g) plain flour
4 teaspoons baking powder

**1.** Set oven at 210°C/425°F/Gas 7. Grease an 8 × 11 inch (20 × 27.5 cm) Swiss roll tin. Place onion and pepper in a medium saucepan with butter or margarine plus peas (or courgettes). Cover pan and cook until all are soft but not mushy. Remove from heat and cool.
**2.** Add the cheese to the cold vegetables in the pan with herbs and seasoning. Stir in the yogurt. Sift the flour and baking powder into the mixture, folding in carefully but thoroughly to make a soft dough. Tip into prepared tin, dust with flour to make less sticky, and pat out evenly. Bake for 12–15 minutes until well risen and golden. Cut into 16–20 squares or fingers when cold.

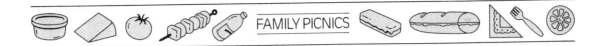
# Barbecue Marinades

You can barbecue the food at home if you like, then wrap in foil and newspaper and pack in insulated boxes or bags (they can be used for hot *or* cold contents). Foods for barbecuing do not have to be expensive – cheaper cuts of meat are good if well cooked. Marinate all meat for 4–24 hours for better flavour. Foil-wrapped fish with herbs, quartered peppers, large mushrooms, small onions and tomatoes can be cooked, and garlic bread heated too.

**Pineapple Sweet-Sour** 5 tablespoons pineapple juice, 2 tablespoons soy sauce, 1 teaspoon grated fresh ginger, 1 tablespoon vinegar, 2 tablespoons brown sugar, and pepper. Combine and use for chicken, pork chops, sausages, fingers of lean boned belly of pork, spare ribs, beef steaks and kebabs.

**Mint and Honey** 3 tablespoons grapefruit juice, 2 tablespoons chopped mint or mint sauce, 1 tablespoon honey, 1 tablespoon vinegar, and pepper. Combine and use for lamb chops, cutlets, kebabs and lean breast of lamb.

**Greek Marinade** 5 oz (150 g) carton plain yogurt, 1 tablespoon lemon juice, 1 clove of garlic, crushed, 2 teaspoons oregano, salt and pepper. Combine and use for chicken, trout, lamb, beef steaks and kebabs.

**Red Wine** 1 glass red wine, 1 clove of garlic, crushed, 1 small onion, chopped, 2 tablespoons olive oil, ½ teaspoon mixed herbs, plenty of freshly ground black pepper, 1 teaspoon mustard. Combine and use for beef steaks, sausages, pork, ham, kebabs and chicken.

**Paprika Marinade** 4 tablespoons ketchup, 3 teaspoons mild paprika, ½ teaspoon hot paprika or pinch of Cayenne, 2 tablespoons soured cream. Combine and use for chicken, trout, pork, lamb or beef cuts.

# Ginger Cake Slab

Like many gingerbreads this improves with keeping, so make 3–4 days in advance. As a traditional end to a picnic meal, serve with a slice of Cheddar or Lancashire cheese or a crisp apple. Do not open oven halfway through cooking or gingerbread will sink in centre.

12 PIECES

**4 oz (115 g) butter or sunflower margarine**
**3 oz (90 g) soft light brown sugar**
**8 oz (225 g) golden syrup**
**¼ pint (150 ml) unsweetened orange juice**
**1 large egg**
**4 oz (115 g) wholemeal flour**
**1½ teaspoons ground ginger**
**1 teaspoon mixed spice**
**½ teaspoon bicarbonate of soda**

**1.** Set oven at 180°C/350°F/Gas 4. Grease a roasting tin and line base with paper. Warm butter or margarine and sugar in medium saucepan. Place tin of syrup on kitchen scales, check weight, then spoon out 8 oz (225 g) into pan and avoid messy weighing. Stir syrup into warm butter/sugar mixture in pan, then add orange juice and egg and leave to cool.
**2.** When cold beat wholemeal flour into pan. Place remaining items in a sieve together then sift through onto mixture and fold quickly with a plastic spatula or metal spoon to evenly mix. Turn into prepared tin and bake for 1 hour or until firm and spongy when pressed in centre. Cool and transport in cooking tin or cut into twelve squares and store in cake tin.

# Fruit and Nut Bars

A great refresher for hungry hikers and bikers. Wrap individual bars in foil to tuck in a pocket. They're also useful to quell hunger pains on the car journey to the picnic spot.

10–12 BARS

**3½ oz (100 g) sunflower margarine**
**7 oz (200 g) digestive biscuits**
**5 oz (150 g) raisins**
**3½ oz (100 g) chocolate chips**
**3½ oz (100 g) chopped mixed nuts or hazelnuts**
**14 oz (400 g) can condensed milk**

**1.** Set oven at 180°C/350°F/Gas 4. Put margarine in an 8 × 11 (20 × 27.5 cm) Swiss roll tin or small roasting tin. Place in the oven to melt. Place biscuits in polythene bag and roll into crumbs with rolling pin. Sprinkle crumbs evenly over base of tin, scatter with raisins then chocolate chips and lastly nuts.
**2.** Pour the condensed milk onto the top of the nuts, trickling evenly over. Bake for 20–25 minutes until golden brown all over. Leave to cool in the tin for 5–10 minutes. Cut into 10–12 bars with an oiled knife while still warm. Wrap in foil when cold.

# Children's Picnic Parties

Coping with children's parties in a confined space is always something of a challenge. Whether celebrating a birthday or not, if you can arrange picnic parties in the long summer holidays, you will be very popular with your friends for taking the children off their hands. (But it's always wise to check what is on at the local cinema in case the weather lets you down, or find a really entertaining film to video.)

Advance planning makes all the difference. Plan the picnic site first: the garden, zoo or local park. If your party is for toddlers, invite all the mothers too. If for small children, of six or less, ensure plenty of adult help (about one grown-up to six children). Two to three girls of nine to twelve can be a great support and enjoy themselves too. (If you are going to the countryside with a gaggle of small children, check where public conveniences are in advance.) Picnic parties for older children are usually best with a set theme – cricket, football, rounders in the park, a visit to the zoo, a swim at the beach or a pool, a nature trail or treasure hunt in the woods or countryside – and you should ask them to come in casual clothing. Organising transport may limit your numbers, but remember a bus or train ride will be a novelty for some children, or arrange that your willing helpers are car drivers and can each collect and return your guests.

Dishing out food and drinks to clamouring children can quickly leave you fraught. Pour out paper cups of drinks and set on a firm surface – back of hatch-back car, a tray or wall, then call the children and hand out before giving any food. Hand the food out after the children have finished this to avoid spills.

If you are going somewhere by car or merely picnicking in the garden, get small cardboard cake boxes from your local bakery or pretty boxes from your stationery shop. Pack a separate *named* box attractively for each child, with small packets of sandwiches wrapped in clingfilm, buns or slices of cake, biscuits, gingerbread men, fruit cartons of jelly or mousse, plastic spoon and, if you like, packets of crisps, sweets, balloons to blow up and a small toy. They can take these boxes home with any prizes or slices of birthday cake added.

If using public transport, pack a named and decorated white paper bag for each child. Choose food that will travel with ease – foil packets of sandwiches, dried fruit, gingerbread men, apples, satsumas, biscuits, sweets, crisps, etc – and which will be easy to carry in a large basket and quick to hand out. Pack a carton or can of drink each separately if you think they will tear the bags, and hand out straws from the packet so they do not crush.

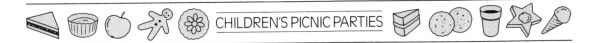 

# Food Necklaces

Colourful, tasty, and just as much fun for children to make as to receive. Aim at a wide variety of ingredients for both a more attractive necklace and more interesting diet, combining sweet and savoury items. Use a large darning needle with 32 inches (80 cm) embroidery thread or wool for each necklace. Slip on a good variety of items and knot ends together. Keep each in a poly-thene bag so they do not tangle. They are ideal for a treasure hunt or nature trail picnic party, as the children can eat as they go, and then sit down for pud or cake (and a rest) at the end.

**Fresh fruit** Cherries (not black, which will stain clothes), black and green grapes, whole clementines or satsumas, apricots, small apples or banana.

**Dried fruit** Raisins, sultanas, pineapple, paw paw, apple rings, apricots and peach.

**Vegetables** Slices of carrot and cucumber, sticks of celery, diced pepper, whole mange-tout peas, tiny tomatoes, sprigs of raw cauliflower.

**Sweets and biscuits** Jelly tots, jelly babies, marshmallows, polos, biscuits with holes in (not chocolate coated which will melt and be messy), small packets of sweets.

**Savoury items** Pretzels, Edam or processed cheese cubes, tiny frankfurters, Hula-Hoops and other packet savoury items.

**Nuts** Whole peanuts in shells, chunks of fresh coconut, unblan-ched almonds, pecan and walnut halves. (Whole nuts not recom-mended for children of six and under at parties.)

# Pretty Party Sandwiches

Children will only be interested in sandwiches if they look pretty and interesting. Mild flavoured low-fat curd or cream cheese is an ideal basic filling which can be flavoured and coloured for variety. Keep to one- or two-bite size. Pack sandwiches by arranging on paper plates, cover tightly with clingfilm, then two to three plates can be stacked up, or place two to three sandwiches in paper cases in party boxes.

**Cress tubs** Cut thick sliced brown bread into 1 inch (2.5 cm) rounds with a cutter. Pipe on circle of cheese, flavoured and coloured with Marmite. Tuck in tiny sprigs of cress and pack in paper cake cases.

**Catherine wheels** Cut crusts off two thin slices of white bread. Mix cheese with tomato purée to colour and flavour. Spread thickly on both slices of bread. Set end to end on clingfilm or foil, roll up together like a Swiss roll – wrap firmly and chill. Cut each across into six pinwheels.

**Super stars** Spread bread with cheese. Cut with star-shaped cutter, sprinkle with multi-coloured hundreds and thousands.

**Daisies** Cut bread with small plain round or fluted cutter. Pipe cheese on with plain pipe in petal shapes. Set yellow or green smarties in centre of each or small rounds of yellow cheese for centre of flower.

**Neapolitan sandwiches** Use two slices of thin brown bread and one of white. Flavour and colour some cheese with tomato purée and some with chopped parsley or cress. Spread each slice of brown bread thickly with one filling and sandwich with white in centre. Chill well, cut off crusts and cut into eight small brick shapes.

# Gingerbread Men

Always beloved of children, but many adults have a nostalgic weakness for them too! This dough is easy to handle, does not spread in cooking, and is perfect for hot little hands that want to help.

12–13 LARGE MEN

**4 oz (115 g) soft light brown sugar**
**3 oz (90 g) sunflower margarine**
**4 oz (115 g) golden syrup**
**10 oz (275 g) flour**
**2 teaspoons ground ginger**
**1 teaspoon bicarbonate of soda**
**Currants for eyes and buttons**

**1.** Set oven at 180°C/350°F/Gas 4. Place sugar and margarine in a saucepan. If scales are available weigh can of syrup and remove 4 oz (115 g) or use 2 large tablespoons. Very gently warm sugar, margarine and syrup until mixture melts but is not hot, only tepid. Sift in the flour with ginger and bicarbonate of soda. Stir together with a spatula or spoon to make a well mixed dough.
**2.** Roll out half the dough at a time on a lightly floured work top to the thickness of 2 × 10 p pieces. Cut out with gingerbread man or other shaped cutter, and place on baking tray using fish slice. Return trimmings to warm pan and knead together for re-rolling. Use five currants for eyes and buttons on each man. Bake for 10–12 minutes or until an even deep golden brown. Leave to cool on tray until beginning to harden then remove to cooling rack.

# Chocolate Granola Crispies

Chocolate crispies are always such a great party favourite it would be a pity to miss these out. Suitable granola type breakfast cereals are Harvest Crunch and Allisons.

16–20 CRISPIES

**3½ oz (100 g) chocolate
1 tablespoon honey
1 oz (30 g) butter
8 oz (225 g) granola
Paper cases**

**1.** Break chocolate up and place in bowl with honey and butter. Set the bowl over a pan of boiling water, then remove pan from the heat immediately. Leave bowl of chocolate on pan to melt without stirring. Prod with a metal spoon and only when completely melted, stir gently to combine ingredients.
**2.** Fold in granola until thoroughly coated, then spoon into paper cases and leave to set.

# Chocolate Ice Cream

Guaranteed a real winner with a real chocolate flavour, this recipe is especially designed for children, using evaporated milk not cream. (You will find it very popular with adults too.) Don't plan to serve this if you are picnicking *too* far from home!

SERVES 12–15

**14 oz (410 g) can evaporated milk**
**4 tablespoons cocoa powder**
**4 tablespoons hot water**
**4 eggs, separated**
**7 oz (200 g) caster sugar**
**Ice cream cones**

**1.** Chill the milk really well, then it will whisk to a thick texture. Stir together cocoa and hot water to make a smooth soft paste then mix in the egg yolks.
**2.** Whisk egg whites to a stiff snow then whisk in sugar a tablespoonful at a time to make a thick meringue-like mixture. Whisk evaporated milk in a separate bowl to a thick mousse. Lastly mix a little egg white with the cocoa paste to make it softer. Fold all three mixtures together carefully, until just evenly mixed. Turn into a large carton to freeze.
**3.** For transportation wrap thickly in newspaper and return to freezer for 24 hours, then place in insulated freezer bag or box, or spoon into well chilled Thermos just before departure. Serve in ice-cream cones.

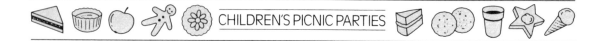
# Party Cake

A cake that will last the journey, will not melt in a hot car and can be packed and unpacked with ease, rules out many old favourites – rich chocolate cakes and other gooey concoctions. You'll need to make sure you have a good strong cake tin or box the right size for your chosen cake.

**1 deep round cake, bought or home-made and any flavour,
or a pair of sandwich cakes
Butter icing of suitable flavour
1–2 packets sponge fingers or *langue de chat* biscuits
1 yard (1 metre) broad coloured ribbon
2–3 boxes Smarties**

**1.** Split and fill deep cake, or sandwich slim cakes together, with a little butter icing. Set on cake board or plate then spread top and side of cake very sparingly.

**2.** Arrange biscuits upright round side of cake, so that they come above the level of the cake. Place the sponge fingers side by side, the *langues de chat* overlapping each other. Tie round ribbon firmly to hold all in place. Place cake on upturned lid of large round cake tin or box and up-turn base over this so you will have no difficulty lifting cake out of a deep tin. *Make sure no one turns the tin over the right way!* Transport Smarties in their boxes ready to tip into your tub-shaped cake when you unpack it. If you wish to use candles set these in place before filling with the layer of Smarties.

# Moveable Feasts

Throughout the year there are a number of social occasions when a really excellent packed meal is required. Whether for a Glyndebourne supper, for Henley Regatta, Wimbledon, Ascot, the Derby, point-to-points or winter shoots, it is more a moveable feast that is required. While many might opt for a Harrods hamper, you may prefer to prepare your own, and I am sure family and friends will appreciate this. As well as the recipes in this chapter, many in Desk-Top Dining will also prove popular.

Decide first whether it is to be table and chair affair or a *déjeuner sur l'herbe*. If you are having to balance a plate and glass, then it is easier to plan a fork lunch or supper plus items you can eat in the fingers. For evening occasions and winter point-to-points or shoots, a hot soup served in a mug will be welcome. Really excellent salads to serve as a starter or with the main course are vital, and most men feel they see too many quiches, and would prefer the Old Vicarage Beef Pie on page 42. Good fruit to finish is hard to beat: strawberries and cream or raspberries, or sliced fresh peaches, nectarines or pineapple with a good splash of liqueur. In winter, if you haven't served a pie first, a fruit flan dessert would be perfect. A conventional serving of cheese will be difficult, so try rolling chunks of Stilton or Lymeswold in chopped walnuts to eat in the fingers.

To pack your moveable feast with style, don't limit yourself to putting food in plastic containers. They aren't elegant and many foods will look much better in shallow heavy dishes covered with clingfilm. Choose big napkins (alfresco eating requires more protection), and good quality paper or plastic plates. I always prefer to use real cutlery.

If there are two cars in the party, try to use one for chairs, tables etc, and the other for food: it is maddening to have to unpack the entire boot to get the table at the bottom. Check the car boot well in advance to remove the spare petrol can (it will flavour the food). A Range Rover with a tailgate makes a marvellous sideboard for dispensing food and drink but any hatch-back is good. Clean it up well first (dog hairs aren't inviting), and line with a large cloth or coloured sheet.

Pack the contents of the boot with some thought, and in the right order. The last thing you need is the cheese (so at the back), and the first things needed are the corkscrew, glasses and drinks. Try to prevent eager volunteers from unpacking the food for you; they can easily reduce your organisation to chaos!

Arrange all the items for the starter in a wicker shopping basket lined with pretty tea towels or tablecloth, which can be lifted out quickly to start the meal. The basket can then be stacked with cutlery and small dirty items as these are finished with. Have a bin bag tucked inside for collecting up rubbish neatly: clutter and confusion do not make for a relaxed atmosphere, so you need to plan the tidy clearing of each course in the meal as well as serving the next.

# Tomato and Dill Soup

A delicious soup for a sophisticated picnic supper when a hot soup is often very welcome (unless you are enjoying a rare heat-wave), and just as good as a warmer for a chilly winter shoot.

SERVES 6

2 medium onions, sliced
2 oz (60 g) butter
2 teaspoons mild paprika
1 tablespoon flour
1 red pepper or cap tinned pimento
15 oz (425 g) can tomatoes
2 tablespoons tomato purée
1¾ pints (1 litre) good chicken stock
1 teaspoon dill
Salt and pepper
5 oz (150 g) carton soured cream

**1.** Cook onion in butter until soft and transparent. Stir in paprika and flour then cook slowly for a further 2–3 minutes. Meanwhile quarter and core pepper if fresh and slip under hot grill, skin side up, to blacken and blister skin so that it can be scraped off. Add sliced pepper, tomatoes, tomato purée and stock to pan, bring to boil, and simmer for 10–15 minutes.
**2.** Purée soup, adding dill and seasoning to taste. Reheat and pour into Thermos, packing carton of soured cream separately, so that a spoonful can be added to each mug or bowl on serving.

# Melon with Spiced Ginger Cream

This ginger sauce can be made well in advance and packed in a screw-top jar to serve with halved Ogen or other small melon, or wedges of Honeydew. Buy fresh ginger when you see it, peel and store in freezer. Grate while frozen as required and return remainder to freezer.

SERVES 6

**2 teaspoons grated fresh ginger**
**1 teaspoon mild curry powder or paste**
**3 tablespoons smooth apricot jam**
**4 tablespoons red wine or port**
**1 tablespoon lemon juice**
**¼ pint (150 ml) double cream**
**3 small or 1 large melon**

**1.** Heat together the ginger, curry, jam, red wine or port and lemon juice. Simmer for 1–2 minutes to reduce until syrupy then leave to cool. This may be done several days in advance and stored in a jar in the fridge.
**2.** Stir cream and ginger mixture together. Halve melons, discarding seeds, but do not cut in slices (if Honeydew) until ready to serve. Wrap halves in clingfilm and chill. Cut in slices and spoon spiced ginger cream on portions as you serve.

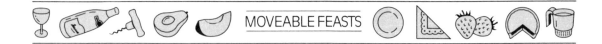 

# Leek and Lymeswold Salad

A colourful and unusual salad, the dressing can be made with any well-flavoured blue cheese. Use as a starter with crisp French bread or brown rolls, or to accompany plain cold meats such as turkey or chicken.

SERVES 6

**1 lb (450 g) leeks, halved lengthwise and washed**
**1 yellow pepper, cored, seeded and cut into strips**
**3 tablespoons milk**
**7 oz (200 g) Lymeswold cheese, diced**
**1 small can pimento**

**1.** Trim any tough dark green leaves off the leeks but keep all those that are tender. Cut into 1 inch (2.5 cm) lengths. Plunge into large pan of boiling salted water for 5 minutes. Add pepper strips to pan of leeks and cook together for a further 2 minutes. Drain and rinse under cold water and leave to cool.
**2.** Warm milk gently in pan, add Lymeswold dice, and crush well with a potato masher to make a smooth dressing. Leave to cool. Cut drained pimento into strips and combine with dressing and vegetables.

# Asparagus, Artichoke and Avocado Salad

A delicious cool green salad to use as a starter or to accompany cold salmon, trout or turkey. Keep cans of both asparagus and artichokes in your store cupboard: you will then never be caught out by unexpected guests or be short of ideas for a sophisticated salad for a Glyndebourne supper or other special occasion. Remember to add the avocado stones to your salad and keep tightly covered with clingfilm: uncover and discard stones just before serving to prevent avocado discolouring.

SERVES 8

**14 oz (400 g) can small asparagus spears**
**14 oz (400 g) can artichoke hearts**
**12 black olives**
**1 small lemon**
**5 tablespoons olive or walnut oil**
**Salt, pepper, mustard and sugar**
**1 avocado (only just ripe)**
**Chopped parsley**

**1.** Drain asparagus spears and artichokes and cut all in half. Halve and stone black olives also. Coarsely grate the rind of lemon or remove in needle shreds then squeeze the juice. Combine juice and oil and season to taste.
**2.** Peel avocado then cut in slices off the stone – a firm pear that is only just ripe will not go mushy when handled. Toss all salad ingredients in dressing carefully and scatter with lemon rind and parsley. Add avocado stones, cover with clingfilm and chill.

# Tongue and Chicken Galette

Your galette will look just like a perfect pressed tongue until you surprise your guests by cutting it like a cake to reveal the different layers. Serve with a variety of salads – the Cumberland Celery Salad (page 60) is particularly delicious.

SERVES 8

**10 slices cooked ox tongue**
**3 lb (1.3 kg) chicken**
**4 tablespoons orange juice**
**1 teaspoon mace**
**Pepper**
**3 slices wholemeal bread**
**1 small onion**
**1 teaspoon fresh chopped sage**
**8–10 oz (225–275 g) ham**

**1.** Set oven at 180°C/350°F/Gas 4. Line a 2 pint (1 litre) soufflé dish or cake tin with four slices of tongue. Cut raw meat from breast of chicken and cut in small fingers. Soak in orange juice with mace and pepper.
**2.** Mince together or purée in a food processor all the remaining chicken cut from the carcass with the bread, onion, sage, ham and six slices of tongue. Work all together and add orange juice drained from chicken breasts. Place a third of the mixture in dish, cover with half of the chicken breast fingers. Proceed with further layer of mixture and remaining breast, and top with remaining mixture.
**3.** Cover with foil, stand dish in a roasting tin with 1 inch (2.5 cm) water in the bottom, and bake for 1½ hours. Chill overnight before turning out.

# Apricot and Almond Flan

Transport in baking tin for safest results. Serve on base of tin slipped onto small round tray or large plate.

SERVES 10–12

**3½ oz (100 g) butter**
**3½ oz (100 g) soft light brown sugar**
**1 egg and 1 yolk, (size 3)**
**4 drops vanilla essence**
**7 oz (200 g) plain flour**

FILLING
**1½ lb (675 g) fresh or frozen apricots**
**3 eggs**
**4 oz (115 g) soft light brown sugar**
**4 oz (115 g) ground almonds**
**2 oz (60 g) very soft butter**
**2–3 tablespoons Cointreau or Kirsch**
**1 oz (30 g) flaked almonds**
**Icing sugar to finish**

1. Thaw the apricots if frozen. Set oven at 180°C/350°F/Gas 4. Allow pastry butter to soften in warm room and beat well. Stir in sugar, egg and yolk, vanilla and, when evenly mixed, fold in the flour to make a firm pastry. Chill well.
2. Halve and stone apricots. Roll out pastry and line a deep 9 inch (27.5 cm) cake tin or 10 inch (30 cm) loose-bottomed flan tin. Cover base with apricots. Separate two of the eggs for the filling. Whisk whites to a snow then whisk in 1 tablespoon sugar. Beat remaining egg and yolks with sugar and almonds to a light mixture, then fold in butter, liqueur and egg whites. Pour over apricots, sprinkle with almonds and bake 40–60 minutes until almond mixture is set. Cool in tin, then dust with icing sugar.

# Mulled Wine

A real reviver for a chilling shoot or Arctic point-to-point. Add brandy as you serve so that guests may have a *dash* or *good splash* according to their preference. If you have been given some rather dubious plonk or home-brewed wine, this is a marvellous way to use it up.

MAKES 12 GLASSES

**2 bottles red Burgundy**
**1 orange**
**½ lemon**
**12 cloves**
**3–4 small slices peeled root ginger**
**1 stick cinnamon**
**½ teaspoon nutmeg**
**2–3 tablespoons brown sugar**

**1.** Heat wine in saucepan with sliced orange, lemon and spices. When moderately hot, turn into a covered bowl and leave for 2 hours or overnight to absorb flavour.
**2.** Strain infused wine back into pan and sweeten to taste. Reheat until very hot but not boiling and pour into Thermos flasks. Pour into glasses or mugs and lace with brandy.

# Index

Apple juice with cloves (hot) 29
Apple mousse, Blackberry and 46
Apple, pear and vine salad 67
Apple salad, Cumberland celery
    and 60
Apple soup, Lentil, celery and 73
Apricot and almond flan 93
Artichokes with broad beans and
    bacon dip 55
Asparagus, artichoke and avocado
    salad 91

Bacon chowder 36
Bacon loaf, Beef and 24
Bacon Tart, Chicken, pea and 45
Banana bread, Date and 48
Barbecued chicken 63
Barbecue marinades 77
Barbecue picnics 72
Beach picnics 72
Bean, bacon and pasta salad 38
Beef and bacon loaf 24
Beef pie, Old Vicarage 42
Blackberry and apple mousse 46
Blackcurrant juice with cinnamon
    (hot) 29
Brown rice and lentil salad 58

Cakes and loaves 12
    Chocolate and hazelnut loaf 28
    Chocolate granola crispies 84
    Date and banana bread 48
    Fruit and nut bars 79
    Ginger cake slab 78

Gingerbread men 83
Hi-fi fruit loaf 66
Party cake 86
Pineapple and sultana cake 49
Celery and apple soup, Lentil, 73
Chicken coleslaw, Tarragon and 62
Chicken galette and tongue 92
Chicken, Lime barbecued 63
Chicken liver spread 21
Chicken Maryland 39
Chicken, pea and bacon tart 45
Children's picnic parties 80–6
Children's favourites 23
Chocolate and hazelnut loaf 28
Chocolate granola crispies 84
Chocolate ice cream 83
Crunchy munchy chicken Maryland
    39
Cumberland, celery and crisp apple
    salad 60

Date and banana bread 48
Desk top dining 52–69
Dill mousse, Salmon and 74
Dill soup, Tomato and 88
Dips 10
    Bacon dip with artichokes and
        broad beans 55
Dressings 10, 11
Drinks 9, 26, 29, 87
    For school children 29
    Mulled wine 94

Equipment 7–10, 71, 87

Insulated bags and boxes 8, 9
Lunch boxes 8
Picnic hampers 8
Plastic bags and boxes 7–11
Thermos flasks 7, 8, 11, 12, 29

Family picnics 70–9
Flans and tarts 12
    Chicken, pea and bacon tart 45
    Mushroom flan 44
    Wholemeal spinach flan 65
Food necklaces 81
Freezing picnic food 10–13
Fruit jelly salads 37
Fruit loaf, Hi-fi 66
Fruit and nut bars 79

Ginger bread men 83
Ginger cake slab 78
Grapefruit juice with honey (hot)
    29

Hazelnut loaf, Chocolate and 28
Hi-fi fruit loaf 66
High energy picnics 72
Horseradish cream, Steak salad
    with 61
Horseradish pâté, Smoked
    mackerel and 56
Hot pepper casserole 64

Insulated bags and boxes 8, 9, 12

Leek and potato soup 20

Lentil and brown rice salad 58
Lentil, celery and apple salad 90
Lentil spread 57
Light-weight picnics 72
Lime barbecued chicken 63
Liver and sausage loaf 43
Low calorie salads for slimmers 37
Lunch boxes 8
Lymeswold salad, Leek and 90

Made-up dishes 11, 12
    Crunchy munchy chicken
        Maryland 39
    Hot pepper casserole 64
    Lime barbecued chicken 63
    Liver and sausage loaf 43
    Meat loaf 24
    Old Vicarage beef pie 42
    Pizza slice 40
    Sausage, apple and sage plait 41
    Tongue and chicken gallette 92
Melon with spiced ginger cream 89
Menus for one month
    Small children 30–1
    Older children and students
        50–1
    Desk top dining 68–9
Mousses
    Blackberry and apple 46
    Orange 25
    Salmon and dill 74
Moveable feasts 87–94
Mulled wine 94

Nut bars, Fruit and 79

Older children and students 32–51
Old Vicarage beef pie 42
Orange juice with ginger (hot) 29
Orange mousse 25

Party cake 86
Pasta salad, Bean, bacon and 38
Pâté 10
    Chicken liver spread 21
    Lentil spread 57
    Smoked mackerel and
        horseradish pâté 56
Peanut butter, Home-made 22
Pear and cinnamon crumble 47

Pear and vine salad, Apple, 67
Pear pie 27
Picnics, family 70–9
Pineapple and sultana cake 49
Pineapple jelly cream 26
Pitta pockets 53
Pizza slice 40
Plastic bags and boxes 7–11
Potato soup, Leek and 20
Pretty party sandwiches 82
Puddings 13
    Apricot and almond flan 93
    Blackberry and apple mousse 46
    Chocolate ice cream 85
    Orange mousse 25
    Pear and cinnamon crumble 47
    Pear pie 27
    Pineapple jelly cream 26

Salads 9–11
    Apple, pear and vine salad 67
    Asparagus, artichoke and
        avocado salad 91
    Bean, bacon and pasta salad 38
    Children's favourites 23
    Cumberland celery and crisp
        apple salad 60
    Fruit jelly salads 37
    Leek and Lymeswold salad 90
    Lentil and brown rice salad 58
    Low calorie salads for slimmers
        37
    Savoury salads 37
    Steak salad with horseradish
        cream 61
    Tabooli 59
    Tarragon and chicken coleslaw
        62
Salmon and dill mousse 74
Sandwiches 9, 10
    Bacon and bean bap 18
    Catherine wheels 82
    Cheese and cucumber roll 18
    Cold pork and coleslaw 18
    Cress tubs 82
    Crunchy bean, nut and curd
        sandwich 18
    Daisies 82
    Double decker varieties 34

Lamb and pea sandwich 18
Mortadella scone 18
Neapolitan sandwiches 82
Pitta pockets 53
Roly poly 33
Russian beef pitta 18
Sardine and tomato sandwich 18
Super stars 82
Sandwich fillings
    American favourite 19
    Chicken liver spread 21
    Crunchy chocolate and banana
        19
    Lemon and walnut 19
    Lime and caerphilly 19
    Peanut butter (home-made) 22
    Pickle and sausage 19
    Spanish omelette 35
    Strawberry and quark 19
    Sultana and apricot curd 19
    Tongue and jelly 19
Sausage, apple and sage plait 41
Sausage loaf, Liver and 43
Savoury scones 76
Sherry soup, Kidney and 84
Small children 17–31
Soups 9, 11
    Bacon chowder 36
    Kidney and sherry soup 54
    Leek and potato 20
    Lentil, celery and apple soup 73
    Tomato and dill soup 88
Spreads 10
    Chicken liver spread 21
    Lentil spread 57
    Smoked mackerel and horseradish
        pâté 56
Stuffed picnic loaf 75
Sultana cake, Pineapple and 49

Tabooli 59
Tarragon and chicken coleslaw 62
Thermos flasks 7, 8, 11, 12, 29
Tomato and dill soup 88
Tomato juice with grated orange
    rind 29
Tongue and chicken gallette 92

Wholemeal spinach flan 65
Wine, mulled 94